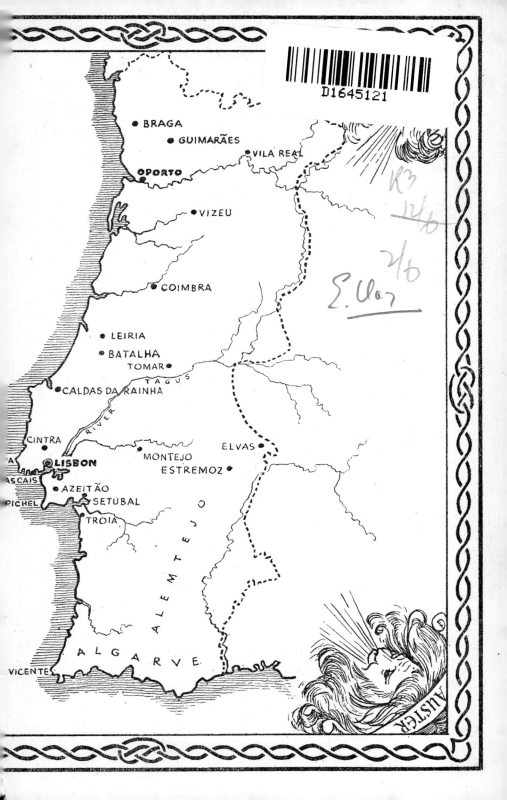

TO PORTUGAL FOR PLEASURE

CINTRA MARKET   [*Frontispiece*

TO PORTUGAL FOR PLEASURE

BY

ALICE FULLERTON

AUTHOR OF "TO PERSIA FOR FLOWERS"

DRAWINGS BY N. EVELYN SANDS

LONDON
GRAFTON & CO.
1945

I DEDICATE THIS
RECORD OF MANY HAPPY MONTHS
TO
BERTIE and OLIVE PELL
WHOSE FRIENDSHIP AND HOSPITALITY
MADE MY VISITS TO PORTUGAL
SO DELIGHTFUL AND EASY

First Published 1945

MADE AND PRINTED IN GREAT BRITAIN BY
MORRISON AND GIBB LTD., LONDON AND EDINBURGH

PREFACE

THESE short sketches are a personal record of two delightful visits to Portugal.

They only tell of things that interested me, and as I go over them in my mind I wish increasingly that I knew more of this charming country, its history, architecture, folklore and flowers. In no way do I pretend to any special knowledge, but I feel that greater knowledge would yield great results, and my regret is that the war cut short my search after the unusual and out of the way. There are many gaps in my narrative. I have made no attempt to describe the well-known sights. I have left those to the guide-books. I have written as I wandered from place to place, always to find something that interested and enthralled me. And I have tried to model myself on Dr. Johnson's Portuguese traveller who " has amused his readers with no romantick absurdity, or incredible fictions ; whatever he relates, whether true or not, is at least probable ; and he who tells nothing exceeding the bounds of probability, has a right to demand that they should believe him who cannot contradict him. He appears by his modest and unaffected narration, to describe things as he saw them, to have copied nature from life, and to have consulted his senses, not his imagination. He meets with no basilisks that destroy with their eyes, his crocodiles devour their prey without tears, and his cataracts fall from the rocks without deafening the neighbouring inhabitants."[1]

I hope my Portuguese friends will take this book as an affectionate tribute to Portugal, to her beauty and her kindness, also of admiration for what she has done in the past, as well as what she is doing now, to help and succour those from less fortunate countries. She is now the land of refuge, as she was once the land of discovery. Her flag has always been in the van of adventure, pushing the curtain of ignorance away before it. Now it is the sign of safety and help to those that claim it.

Portugal is a gardener's paradise in the spring. This is

---

[1] From the *Life of Samuel Johnson*, by James Boswell, vol. i. p. 62, 6th ed. 1811.

only one of her many attractions, not the least of which is the charming welcome and kindness given to strangers, particularly to the British. To me it is a warm, friendly, happy land—a land of simple pleasures, charming people and beautiful country. It was, when I knew it, as yet unspoiled and unexploited. How long it will remain so is hard to say, for its charms are finding a larger number of admirers every year. I wish I could keep it selfishly for my own pleasure, yet here I am telling others of its delights.

BRIGHTLING, 1945.

CONTENTS

I. My Love of Portugal is Born   9

II. South of the Tagus   24

III. Blessing the Cod-fish Fleet   30

IV. Santo Antonio da Ussa   35

V. Processions and Witches   42

VI. "Mercados" or Markets   52

VII. Bulls and Bull-fights   58

VIII. "Quintas" and Gardens   64

IX. Plants and Plant-collecting in Portugal   82

X. The Story of Portugal   90

LIST OF ILLUSTRATIONS

Cintra Market   *Frontispiece*

FACING PAGE

Evora Monte   24

Leiria   24

Codfish Fleet   32

Santo Antonia Da Ussa   32

Basin in Old Kitchen at Manique   32

Fountain at Arraiolos   56

Fountain at Montemor   56

Fish Women at Nazaré   60

Field Workers   60

Campinos   60

Owner of Bulls   60

Mateus, near Vila Real   64

Moorish Pavilion at Bacalhoa   64

Bacalhoa   96

Fountain in Museum Court at Coimbra   96

ACKNOWLEDGMENT

I owe my most grateful thanks to Mrs. N. E. Sands for expressing so well in her drawings what I have tried to put into words, to Miss Marion Jennings for her valuable data on folklore, to Captain Collingwood Ingram for his help in my chapter on Portuguese flora, to Miss Malherbe who has done so much of the dull and necessary revision of this book, and to my friends in Portugal who have helped me with other details.

I

MY LOVE OF PORTUGAL IS BORN

I FIRST saw Lisbon on a hot September day. David and I stood on the deck of the *Alcantara* as she turned in a wide sweep round Cabo da Roca past Cascais, over the bar with the solid tower of Belem on our left, Lisbon on the hills beyond and the far shore of the Tagus almost hidden by haze. I remember little about our landing, only the great heat and the difficulty of making myself understood or of understanding what was said to us.

We had hoped to go to Monte Estoril at once, but found all Portugal was there before us, so sadly went to the Avenida Palace in Lisbon. The heat stifled me and I hoped we would soon get away.

David hung from the windows till late at night, watching the passing crowds, who did not seem to think night was meant for rest. Finally quiet reigned, to be suddenly broken by what we thought were gunshots.

" Quick, Mother, come and look ! It must be another revolution," said David, rushing to throw open the shutters, bent on missing nothing. Yet more shots, but there was something queer about them, for though they made a great noise there was also light and the air was full of falling stars.

The revolution dissolved itself into a fine rocket display to advertise the bull-fight on the following Sunday.

This is my first memory of Portugal, when President Carmona had just come into power. This memory and one other stayed with me for eleven years, until I returned.

The second memory was sitting on my luggage in the shade, exhausted by a long, hot train journey. I was waiting till David returned with some conveyance which would take us to Busaco. We had got out at the wrong station and were miles away. The heat was terrific and beat up from the red earth and white road in front of me. Near by an old man crouched, covered by a huge cape. He seemed to be asleep and certainly oblivious of me. Suddenly he arose quietly and disappeared round the corner. I

sat gasping in the heat and wondering how long it would be
before David returned. There was a movement at my side and
I looked up to see the old man. In his hands he held some vine
leaves and on them were two large bunches of grapes, one black
and one white. " Would the senhora accept them ? She looked
tired and hot. Oh no, he was proud to give them to her ; it was
a pleasure for him to do anything for an Englishwoman." And
so my real love of Portugal was born.

In March 1938 I again sailed up the Tagus, this time from
Egypt, to join friends at the American Legation.

The port had changed greatly, with its new docks, ship-
building yards and many ships. The city lay above it all, its
windows reflecting the morning sun. In one place, above the
houses, in what I afterwards came to know was the Legation
Quarter, flew the great red, white and black flag of the Nazis.
The docks were crowded and were packed with rows and rows
of huge lorries, crates and, next to them, rows of cars, while the
river was full of cargo boats. There seemed little room for our
liner and her passengers.

It was early morning, but there on the dock was the tall figure
of my host. Behind him was the Legation car with its Stars and
Stripes waving from the bonnet. While officials were still busy
chattering, I was called. The U.S. Minister had come aboard,
and would I go at once ? Joseph, the chancery clerk, took my
passport and luggage receipt and I left before any of the other
passengers had landed, rather breathless and feeling very grand.

My feeling of importance was rather reduced later on when
Joseph apologetically asked for information about the Russian
visa on my passport. In those days of the Spanish Civil War,
Russia was *persona non grata* in Portugal. Why had I, seemingly
so respectable, been to Russia, and as shortly before as 1935 ?

I explained to Joseph that I had spent six days in the train
crossing Russia on my way to Persia, that I had done so as it
was the cheapest as well as the quickest way to get to Persia,
but Bertie Pell, the Minister, had to vouch that I was not a
Bolshevik in disguise before I got my *permis de séjour*.

The Legation Quarter in Lisbon stands high, overlooking
the river and its teeming life. The docks were hidden by the
houses lower down the slope below the American Legation, which
towered above them all. Facing us was the Belgian Legation.

the house of the British Counsellor and beyond, round a corner, the huge German Legation. When I returned there in 1939 I found that the Germans had concentrated in a circle round this, and the end of our street was little more than a German settlement. They had many more officials and clerks than the year before.

The British Embassy lay below us. Our Government had short-sightedly refused to buy all the land that was beyond and below it, so that now it was surrounded by many buildings and working-class flats, where there might have been a large garden. What garden there is, is charming, but I fancy the whole Embassy is far too small for its growing needs.

. The most beautiful of all the legations is the French. The French Government rightly think that, as part of their national property, their legations and embassies should represent some of the consequence and beauty of their country. In Lisbon their legation in the Palace of Dom Sebastian is full of fine tapestries and French furniture. Its terraced gardens overlook the ancient port and river.

Dom Sebastian the Desired, a tragic figure, sailed in 1578 with his knights to conquer the Moors in Morocco. He and his forces were routed in the battle of Alcazar Kebir, after which he was never seen again, dead or alive. There are many legends about him, and in the great cool rooms, with their wonderful tapestries and *objets d'art*, one feels as if all that has passed since his day was a dream, and that he is still watching with amused and detached eyes the life that passes as a play before him. That there was some definitely deep feeling of the past in the palace was the strongest impression that I had when, alone at night, watching the moon from the terrace, the docks and ugly buildings seemed to fade away and the river was full of many-masted galleons. There were cries of men, the clank of armour and the sound of horses. Back in the light of the *salon* it took me some time to forget the feeling. I half expected the great doors to open and the Crusader knights to enter, come to fetch their king. I knew that the Minister's wife was very conscious of this undercurrent from another world at the Legation, and continually felt the presence of some unseen visitor. It made such a deep impression on her that when she wrote a charming study of Dom Sebastian she felt she had been inspired by some outside influence.

The French Minister and his wife—the *Amé Leroys*—were an extremely clever and delightful couple. He had been Briand's secretary and took his work in Portugal very seriously. He had a hard row to hoe, as feeling was still anti-French. It had been so in some quarters since the Peninsular Wars, and the feeling was increased by the actions of the Blum Government. Before I left in May 1939 Monsieur Leroy told me that at last things were better. His hard work had shown results, and when the French battleship *Dunkerque* and her satellite cruiser came on their official visit, the entire town turned out to welcome them. The procession of French sailors and marines from the docks to the Cenotaph was watched by enthusiastic crowds, who clapped and cheered them.

Shortly afterwards at a big party at the British Embassy I saw Monsieur Leroy in deep and animated conversation with both Dr. Salazar and President Carmona. I watched these two men with the deepest interest. The President is a fine old soldier, upright and active in spite of his seventy years. He was in uniform, his chest covered with medals, and stood surrounded by all the great people of his administration. They and the diplomats wore much be-medalled uniforms. Amongst them Dr. Salazar stood out in his black suit with not a ribbon to liven it, his face quiet but keen and intent, listening to what was said to him, yet, it seemed to me, missing nothing of his surroundings. One felt the power of his concentration and will, and his incorruptible detachment from the world showed in his face.

The arrival of the French ships was the occasion for many official and private ceremonies, all of which were gall and wormwood to the Germans. The British fleet had paid an official visit to Lisbon before I arrived, and the German Minister, Baron Hoyningen-Huene, asked that the German fleet should have an official reception too, but he was told that the Portuguese would not welcome them so soon after the Nazis had marched into Prague.

The Minister insisted that his ships should come to Lisbon. "The German people will not understand it if they do not." But he was told that it could only be an unofficial visit.

The day after the French ships left, the pocket-battleship *Deutschland* steamed up the river, followed by her supply ship and a small cruiser. Whereas the two French ships had swung at anchor in mid-stream, the *Deutschland* could tie up to the dock, and in contrast she seemed very small. The town was quickly invaded by her sailors. Unlike their country people, who came on the *Kraft-durch-Freude* ships, these men had money to spend. They were given a special allowance so that they could make a splash while in Lisbon.

Feeling was very strong about the Germans, and people were extremely nervous. They were not helped by the obvious anxiety of the Axis partner, Italy, and the truculent attitude of the German Minister. That they should insist on their ships coming to Lisbon seemed sinister, and many rumours were flying about. Some people even left the environs of the Tagus so as to be out of range of the German guns. This feeling against the Germans was so strong that members of the Legion and other patriotic organizations were given the task of shepherding the sailors about the town to prevent rows, though they were not always successful in doing so, as I heard there were many fights.

In spite of protests the German sailors insisted on marching to the Cenotaph. They were followed by lorries full of police, who also watched from many windows, so I was told, with tear gas ready to use if necessary.

When the *Kraft-durch-Freude* ships came, it was different. Their strange-looking passengers had not a penny to spend. They wandered aimlessly about, looking at the many things in the shops that were, even then, rare in Germany. A few sold their cameras or field-glasses for cash and so were able to buy something. They were odd creatures—red-faced, flaxen-haired, hatless girls and big men. Many of these men were in leather Tyrolean shorts and felt hats with feathers. These ships came regularly every fortnight, sometimes singly, sometimes in pairs.

After the successful visits of the British and French fleets and the failure of his own, the German Minister sent out invitations to a party on a huge ship specially built for these pleasure cruises. Curiosity made me go with the American Legation party.

The ship and her consort had arrived about six that morning. As they steamed to their anchorage the air was split by gunfire. All Lisbon woke with a shock. The Germans had returned to bombard us ! But it was only daylight fireworks sent off to announce their arrival. The sky was full of puffs of smoke which cleared to show parachutes. On the end of each hung either the Swastika or the Portuguese flag. These floated down slowly as irritated people went back to bed and to try to sleep again.

The German party was on the ship *Dr. Ley*, and we got there late. Many of the guests had gone, so that the German Minister could devote himself to his American colleague and show him the wonders of this pleasure liner. I was put in the charge of a tall fair youth, his face deeply scarred by slashes across one cheek. He was one of the German Legation attachés.

The cabins that we were shown were bad, crowded and small, but the companions and saloons were large and fine, and so arranged that by the use of sliding doors almost the whole deck space could be turned into one large room. As the ship was an oil burner, her funnel did not come through the saloons, which gave far more deck space.

Having seen all I could below, I followed the rest up and out on to the games deck.

The whole top of the ship was one huge expanse, except for a small superstructure forward.

" Why, she is an aircraft carrier ! " I exclaimed.

" I assure you, *gnädige Frau*," said a furious voice at my elbow, " she is nothing of the kind," and I turned to see the young attaché, scarlet with rage, glaring at me.

" Well," I answered, " if she's not, she could quickly be made into one."

That night the big liner and her consort pulled out into mid-stream and gave a fine display of fireworks before they sailed. I suppose it was to offset the illuminations of the French fleet, which had given so much pleasure.

My only other contact with the Germans was during the Papal Conclave. The city was aflame with rumours. The people were afraid that their own cardinal might be chosen, for he was deeply loved and venerated and they did not want to lose him. Everyone wondered what effect cardinals from the New World would have on the voting. They were attending the Conclave for the first time in history. (Rumour said that Mussolini and Hitler had sent in a list of names of cardinals who would be *persona non grata* to them.)

There was a big party at the American Legation that night. The German Minister and his wife came, as well as the *Chef de Protocol* of the Portuguese Government.

Before dinner he drew me to one side and said :

" If you want to see something amusing to-night, watch the German's face when I tell his Excellency the American Minister who has been elected Pope to-day."

" What, already ? " I asked, " and who ? "

But he only smiled and put his finger to his lips. Half-way through dinner I caught his glance across the narrow table as he leant forward and said to my host :

" Have you heard, Monsieur le Ministre, that Cardinal Pacelli has been elected Pope this afternoon ? "

Hoyningen-Huene, who was sitting next to my hostess, jumped.

" What ! " he said. His face turned almost grey and for the rest of the meal he never uttered a word, crumbling his bread into pellets with nervous hands.

Very shortly after dinner he excused himself. His wife was not feeling well, he said, and they left.

My Portuguese friend came towards me.

" Well ? " he asked.

I thanked him for warning me, as I had been deeply interested.

The Italians, too, were much affected and, I thought, greatly worried by events in Germany. One night I was sitting at dinner between the Italian naval attaché and Admiral Wode-house, who was head of a British Naval, Military and Air Force Commission in Portugal in 1938.

The Italian could hardly contain himself with pleasure at the recently signed naval agreement between England and Italy. Rubbing his hands together, he chuckled :

" Now we can be friends again, we should always be friends. Britain and Italy always have been—no more trouble between us."

I thought Admiral Wodehouse received these signs coldly.

" I do not trust him an inch," he murmured. " I am not taken in by his gush."

The Italian Minister, Signor Mameli, was charming, but his English wife irritated me as she was far more Italian than the Italians. I could not follow her anti-British attitude nor her continual talking of " You British." I once said to her, " Weren't you British too ? " which stopped her for a moment.

The Mamelis were desperately anxious when the Germans marched into Prague, for they expected trouble. This anxiety was given away by the small girl's English governess, who wailed sadly to her friends at the idea of separation from them, for she would have to leave them if there was war, so we knew they feared the worst.

The Spanish Civil War was still in full swing when I came to Portugal in 1938. Neutral diplomats came and went, bringing back increasing warnings of the Germans' power in Spain. Land was being bought up by " tourists." Key posts in the police, railways, post offices, etc., were being taken over by Germans. One military attaché, though he belonged to what was then an almost Fascist country, now one of our bravest and most terribly persecuted allies, told me that his feelings were more and more anti-Falange as he saw the misery and oppression growing in Spain.

He had no praise for the Reds, whose atrocities and destruction of beauty and of cultural objects had shocked and alienated him, as they had all those who otherwise supported them against the Falange, but he saw what would happen if Franco won.

" Do you not understand," he said, " that all this ridiculous non-intervention acts completely in favour of Franco ? He is very contemptuous of France and England, and he evades the restrictions with the greatest of ease."

He told me that the masses of cars and lorries I had seen on the docks when I arrived were for " civilian Spain ! " They were driven off by men in black coats with the Falange buttons in their lapels. Those streams of cars and lorries going towards Spain were a nightly sight. Returning from south of the Tagus we would meet the convoys, and in the lorries were piled the wooden cases in which they had been packed.

Franco, he said, got all he wanted through the non-intervention blockade, ammunition and explosives " to be used for mines," metal for " sewing machines " and so on through the list of raw materials. Only big guns could not be covered by some civilian need, though most types of aeroplane were.

" Why," he asked, " do you not see what will be the result when Franco wins ? You will have a nation of enemies at your back door in Gibraltar. Either help the Reds—really help them —or really help Franco. Do not preach one thing and by weakness allow the opposite to happen."

He told me that each time he went to Spain he missed some official that he had known. In answer to enquiries a quick sign across the throat suggested what had happened to him. In every case these men had been replaced by Germans. I found the responsible British in Lisbon very concerned by all this and the seemingly hopeless task of getting our Government to see the truth.

There was also a strong Spanish movement for uniting the two countries, Portugal and Spain, under Spanish leadership to form an Iberian block. Though the Portuguese had supported Franco all through the Spanish Civil War, for the initial atrocities of the Reds completely alienated all the sympathy some of them might have had, the old anti-Spanish feeling was still strong, and the Portuguese would have strongly resented and resisted any attack on their independence.

At one party in a neutral house I had pressed into my hand, with great secrecy, several slips of paper. On examining them I found they had the arms of Spain joined to those of Portugal by the Hapsburg eagle. Why I was given them I do not know, but I quickly passed them on to the British Embassy, to Geoffrey Dawson, the editor of *The Times*, who was then in Portugal, and finally to a Portuguese friend, who took her copy to the Portuguese Foreign Office at once, as I suggested. She was told that it was printed by the Communists in Spain.

That there was a very strong wish in Spain for this amalgamation I do know, for, after a letter of mine about Portugal had been printed in the *Spectator*, I was written to and visited by a mysterious man in England, who told me he was part of the organization which hoped to promote the union. He was writing a series of articles about it in (I think) the *Manchester Guardian*, and asked if I thought there was any support for the idea in Portugal. I assured him that from the little I knew there would be none. The Portuguese are intensely nationalistic, independent and rightly proud of their long and glorious history and of their contributions to the geographical knowledge of the world.

At the British Embassy were Sir Walford and Lady Selby.

2

I remember hearing that Sir Walford was to make a speech a short time after he arrived *en poste*. It is a difficult language, and no one expected him to rise as he did and to make a delightful speech in perfect Portuguese. This went straight to the hearts of the Lisbonites, as did his deep interest in the country and his friendship for the people. For the first time for many years the British Embassy was the centre of the diplomatic world. Their chef, who had made their cuisine famous in Vienna, came with the Selbys, and, apart from anything else, the renown of the Embassy food ran through the land and everyone wished the Selbys would stay for ever in Lisbon.

In contrast to some former ambassadors, Sir Walford went everywhere. I was at one Portuguese tea-party where there was only one British woman besides myself, and she the wife of a Portuguese. Lady Selby arrived and with her Sir Walford, who looked with horrified surprise at a women's gathering when he expected mixed company, but he stayed to please his hostess, and won more friends

Lady Selby and I had a great interest in flowers in common, and it was she who told me where to find the lovely little " angels' tears " narcissus, and brought me from Cape St. Vincent the *Scilla* which grows there and nowhere else in the world.

At the Netherlands Legation were the Sillems, lately arrived from Greece, charming and very musical people. Misele Sillem has a beautiful voice, and John plays the viola well. He is a great collector of birds and his knowledge of them is profound. He discovered in Portugal a new finch which, I believe, is called after him. It was with him that I went in search of the elusive blue magpie.

The American Legation is one of the largest in Lisbon, a great square house on the hillside, with a garden at the back, full of arum lilies and flowering shrubs. It was ideal for entertaining, with its large *salons* leading one from another, all reached by a wide staircase.

The American Government, unlike the French and British, does not always think it necessary to own their embassies and legations, and this one is not United States property, nor is it really properly furnished. My host, Herbert Pell, brought everything for it from America, including his family pictures. The result was charming, for Olive Pell has not only taste but knowledge. It is hard on each successive Minister to find a house which an ungrateful State leaves half empty. I feel that the dignity of such a great country as the United States demands an embassy or legation of its own in every capital, with its own furniture and works of art, such as the French always have. The British embassies are fine, but the Office of Works' idea of beauty often stops at crude portraits of Queen Victoria or King George.

Lisbon in 1938–39 was a very different place from the Lisbon I had seen in 1927. It had been cleaned up, and on the out-skirts of the city were built new colonies of small workmen's houses, each with its strip of garden. The hospitals had been greatly improved, and I believe the maternity hospital in Lisbon is one of the best in the world. The prisons I had not seen before, but I did see the women's prisons on my last two visits. The prisoners lived in large, clean, whitewashed buildings, and many of them had children with them. There seemed to be little constraint except for the confining walls, and the women were deeply interested in the industry of carpet-making, which had been started in the prison by various ladies.

In Portugal they make a special type of carpet, which is not woven but worked by coarse wools into sacking. It is an art that has existed for centuries. In the prison they were copying the old designs in the original colours and the carpets could be bought extremely cheaply. This not only gave them something useful to do, but also a little money to save against their release. My hostess got up some concerts for these women and they were given in the centre court of the prison. They crowded the arcade around it and hung from the windows. Though they liked the English songs and piano music, the success of the afternoon was a young Portuguese who sang local songs, playing his own accompaniment. Some were evidently ribald, judging by the laughter and shouts that asked for more. When we left, the prison was humming like a beehive with gusts of talk and laughter, and the next time we went there we were surrounded and plied with questions : " When would the senhoras come and sing again ? "

There are fascinating antique shops all over the town, but in nearly every case the value of the antiques is well known, though Portugal used to be the happy hunting-ground for china collectors. The country was full of the porcelain we erroneously called Lowestoft, but which is really *Compagnie des Indes*. It was brought by the great navigators from China. In the past each house had its fine dinner service, some blue and white, others coloured, but collectors have long ago combed the market. The only hope of finding a treasure was by continually hunting in what were really junk shops. There, hidden amongst piles of rubbish, things were still to be found.

The taxis in the city were practically all British. The Austin Ten seemed to have a monopoly, and they were very suitable for the narrow streets which climb the seven hills on which Lisbon is built. There was one taxi-driver who often took me about, and once he got to know me he shyly asked if I would correct an exercise for him. I found he was teaching himself English and was making heavy weather of the pronunciation. I asked him why English.

" But, Senhora, the English have always been our friends, and so many of them come here. It would be such a good thing if I could tell them about the places I take them to see. The guide-books really do not give enough information."

The students' songs, the *fados*, are something that no one should miss hearing. There are many fashionable places where they can be heard, but, really to enjoy them in the nearest approach to their native setting, go late at night to some café where the clients are students, sailors or working men, for women are seldom if ever seen in these places. The surroundings are simple, and as time goes on, the room fills with a gay, talkative crowd, who sit drinking the local wine and smoking. A small platform at the end of the room is empty. Suddenly the lights are lowered and three people come from behind a curtain. One is a woman wrapped in a magenta shawl. She is a mulatto and, from the applause, is evidently popular. The two men with her have different types of guitars—one, which is called the *guitarra*, on which the tune is played, the other, *viola da Franca*, for the accompaniment of chords.

The woman's voice has the strange, sad tones of the negro mingled with the harsh, vibrant quality of the untrained Southern singer. Starting slowly and with not much feeling, she soon becomes possessed by the passion of sadness in her song, the whole tune alters as she swings, and the rhythm is always mourn-

ful but faster as the story unfolds.   The end comes suddenly and
she seems to wake, as if from a dream, and accept the almost
hysterical acclamation of her audience.   These *fados* are often
heard in the streets, men serenading some inamorata or gathered
together to join in the nostalgic singing.

As Bertie Pell was to be elected a member of the Institute of
Coimbra, we motored there.   It was the first capital of Portugal,
and has the second oldest university in Europe.

When we were shown over the buildings, the first we saw
was the chapter council room.   Here each faculty has its chair
and each chair its special colour.   The colour of the faculty
is repeated in the bunches of ribbon worn on the shoulder of the
student to show which school he is taking for his degree.   Each
faculty has its mace to carry in ceremonies.   These were made
of a beautiful mellow silver in the shape of our great mace, but
with short stems.   I touched one, as the surface gleamed with
such a curious light, unlike that of any other silver I had seen,
and I found, to my surprise, that it was of carved wood.   The
professor who was showing us the university told me the story
of these wooden copies.   In the Peninsular War the French
army came to Coimbra and, finding the ancient and beautiful
silver maces, took them back to France.   " What could we do
but have them copied in silvered wood ? " he asked.   Hearing
of the French looting, the priest of the university chapel managed
to hide the sanctuary lamp and the altar candlesticks.   The lamp
now hangs in the chapel, a beautiful example of work by a
sixteenth-century Portuguese silversmith.   The candlesticks are
there too, but are not so fine.

How the treasure was saved from looting by the French
troops was another story told me in Oporto.   In the great church
of the Sé there is a fine silver triptych and altar front of early
date.   On the steps in front of it are huge candlesticks, about
seven feet high, of fine, massive design, but made of rather dull
pewter.   The story is that when the French occupied Oporto,
the priests at the Sé had time to whitewash the triptych and altar
front, so that they looked like carved plaster.   The great silver
candlesticks standing on the steps could not be hidden nor
whitewashed ;   it was impossible to paint them in the short time
the priests had before the looting forces got to the cathedral.
When they came, the altar and triptych attracted no attention,

but the silver candlesticks were taken away and to-day dull copies stand in their place.

The library at Coimbra is most beautiful. It is divided into two sections, one painted a deep rose-red, the other a dark blue-green. The baroque woodwork and carving are a mellow gold. It is full of treasures. We were shown an enchanting picture book of geography and travel in East Africa in the days of the great Albuquerque and even earlier. Each picture showed a small map of the coast-line with harbours and villages, and all over its pages were drawings of animals and creatures which had been seen or were supposed to live in the various places—lions, tigers, unicorns, strange birds. One wonders if they were drawn from the tales brought back by the adventurous Portuguese, who so bravely went time and time again to Abyssinia and along the East African coast in search of Prester John. Some of these men remained and married natives, and have in Abyssinia to-day descendants who are proud of their Portuguese ancestry.

In the time of Prince Henry the Navigator, Lisbon was not the great port it afterwards became. In early times the Algarve was the clearing-house for the trade to the North. All the wealth of the world poured through its harbours. Prince Henry sent many of his great expeditions from there, and there were many ships which went regularly to the Irish ports and to Bristol amongst other places.

The Algarve had been taken from the Moors ninety years after they had been driven from the North and Lisbon captured in 1147, and perhaps for that reason it was looked upon for a long time as a separate part of the kingdom. The kings were " King of Portugal and the Algarve." Prince Henry lived there for many years, watching the coming and going of his fleets, listening to the tales of his great captains, always planning to discover new territories, add to the greatness of his country and to gain more knowledge. He also kept in touch with the universities in other lands, and scholars were sent to Oxford and Cambridge as well as elsewhere. Galway, on the Irish coast, was in close touch with Portugal, and Prince Henry sent an African lion to the authorities as a present.

It was not until the sixteenth century that the emphasis shifted to Lisbon, and from there the later expeditions set out, such as those of Bartholomew Diaz, Vasco da Gama and Cabral.

From then onwards it was the Tagus as opposed to the bay of Lagos. The Portuguese brought great riches to their beautiful city, for their travels ranged all over the globe from Brazil to Abyssinia, from the Cape of Good Hope to Iceland. They had colonies in India and Siam, and already in those early days Newfoundland was their *terra do Bacalhao*. So Lisbon expanded and grew, though we can see little now of her early past. The earthquake in 1755 destroyed most that was ancient and beautiful.

The great St. Anthony of Padua was born in Lisbon in 1195, and there is the church of Santo Antonio da Sé, which is built on the supposed site of his birthplace, though it only dates from 1812. St. Anthony is the beloved patron of all Portuguese, and they do not like his being called " of Padua." " Why, he is *our* saint, born here and lived here for many years before he went to teach in Italy and France." His statue is often seen wearing a red sash. An old custom was to adopt saints into the army, and they were given the honorary rank of an officer. During the Peninsular Wars England thought it would be a graceful gesture to enrol St. Anthony in our army as well, without pay of course, and the red sash is part of the uniform of a field officer of that date. There is a tale that a bishop for many years drew St. Anthony's salary as an officer in the Portuguese army !

These glimpses of old and new Portugal so interested me that I felt I was no longer content to see only what was visible on the surface or to the ordinary tourist. I wanted to know more of the country, its proper history and works of art. The more I learned, the more I found of interest and the greater were the fields for study which opened before me.

II

SOUTH OF THE TAGUS

PORTINHO lay below us, a cluster of tiny, fishermen's huts, with a primitive inn, and one surprisingly modern house edging the sandy curve of the beach. The hills around were thick with shrubs in flower, pink, mauve and yellow. The white walls of Arrabida Convent crowned one hill, its empty cells and chapel full of light and sunshine, and its terraces a blaze of colour— for though it is empty, the convent is still cared for, and it looked as if it were expecting friends at any moment to fill its many rooms.

On the cliff over the bay stood the tiny pension, a square block of grey stone with loopholed bastions at the four corners— an old fort converted. The walls were covered with a deep purple bougainvillea growing through the tall scarlet geraniums at its foot. The soft air was like velvet and the sea and sky were a vivid blue, reflecting one another. Across the horizon small fishing tugs went to and fro, dragging their nets behind them, and on the sea below the cliff were several long boats with curved prow and stern, going from one lobster pot to another.

We stopped at the pension to ask if we could stay there. The two little maids eagerly showed us the three or four bedrooms which were small, bare and clean. One had a large balcony where stood an ancient cannon facing out to sea. In front of the entrance, sheltered from the road by a high wall, was a long terrace shaded by a pergola of vines and covered with little tables and chairs. Over its side we looked straight down to the sea below.

It was early April and customers were few and far between. The yearly clean-up of the house was in progress. On the terrace stood rows of wire wash-basin stands, with a jug and pail beside them ; a man was carefully rubbing some of them with sandpaper, while a second painted others bright green and white.

The little maids were eager to have us as guests, but the host was not there. He lived in the nearest townlet, and it was he who settled who should stay at his inn. Would the honourable

LEIRIA

EVORA MONTE

senhoras deign to go back a few miles and see him ? He would indeed be honoured by the visit of such distinguished ladies, they said, looking with awe at the flag and diplomatic sign on our car.

We retraced our steps up the long road which wound in and out of the hills, and found the innkeeper. He came out to us, fat and smiling. " Our visit would be a great compliment to his house—everything would be done for our comfort—a bath— well, there was none at the moment, but one would be provided if we would wait till the morrow. The cost would be 5s. a day, and included wine, but not drinking water, which was an extra. This he would provide in gallon bottles labelled with our name so that no one should drink it but us."

Our rooms had neither carpets nor curtains. The beds were narrow and the pillows and mattresses made of straw. Wash-basin stands and jugs were brought in for us, still sticky with new paint, and candles to light us at night. I carried a small oil lamp with me, which was received with cries of approval, but questioning looks. Had the senhora oil for the lamp ? Then all was well, for they had none to spare and more would not be fetched till the next day.

The terrace was filled for supper by a motley crowd, a few travellers like ourselves, many men in working clothes, and a family with three very small children, who ate everything they could get and drank large glasses of wine and water. Their mother seemed quite casual about them, but the father busied himself by keeping their plates filled while eating the contents of his own ; his waistcoat was covered by a large red napkin tied round his neck. The supper was of thick vegetable soup, fresh sardines, which had been brought to the door half an hour before—we had watched the bargaining and discussion that went on when they were bought—meat covered with a paste of vegetables, cheese and good coffee. The wine was thin and sour, but most refreshing when mixed with water from the large straw-bound bottle that stood beside us.

Our night was comfortable, the linen coarse but clean, and breakfast was of coffee, coarse wholemeal bread and butter.

Later, as we were starting for the hills, with a great noise of horn and engine, our host's car appeared, an old closed coupé, and perched on the top was a colossal tin bath almost the size of a coffin and half again as high. This was for the two senhoras who had so insistently asked for it yesterday. The whole household turned out to get it down and into the house. The front door was too narrow—perhaps the back one would be better. No, that also was too small. It looked as if it would sit for ever on the terrace. However, one bright youth suggested another plan. With great difficulty it was tied up, slung out over the cliffside and brought to my window. Victory ! It fitted, and with much labour and shouting it was gradually lowered and put in the middle of the floor (where it took up half the space of my tiny room, touching my bed, with a narrow passage on the far side). The men looked at me curiously, wondering how I would get into it, I suppose. " These strange foreigners," I could hear them say. " Why did they want such things as a bath when the sea was just below ? "

All that day, as I climbed over the hills flower-hunting, I thought of the nice hot bath I would have that night, but alas ! two inches of warm water was the allowance reluctantly given me—far more, I was told, than the other guests would use in a week. The next problem was how to empty it afterwards. As there was no plug-hole, the maids, bent nearly double, ladled out what water they could, and finally the entire household united in lifting it to tip the remainder into a pail, wiping their damp foreheads afterwards from the exertion. Such a commotion did it cause that I gave up all thoughts of a bath for myself in the future, and decided to use it as a receptacle for plants, baskets or anything I wanted put out of the way. There it sat, a monument to the unnecessary luxuries we ask for in and out of season and place.

Above Portinho there is a great new road. It was unfinished when I went over it last ; only its rough foundation had been cut out of the Arrabida hills and over their summits. At first it overlooks the convent and the tiny bay below. As it rises, the view is breath-taking. On one side the green slopes fall sharply to the deep-blue sea, and in the distance the long point of Troia, with its Phœnician and Roman remains, breaks the line of sea and sky. On the other, the great ruined castle of Palmella lies across a deep valley, which is a patchwork of green crops and deep-red earth. Beyond again is the lowland to the Tagus, and in the distance, behind the hills of Lisbon, is a misty outline, the escarpment of Cintra, where the Montes Claros range ends in a sharp break of falling rocks at the edge of the sea.

Legend says that here, beyond the sharp line of rock and cliff, lay Atlantis, joined to the mainland by the now-broken ridge of the Monte Claros. I know this is contrary to all the traditions of mythical Atlantis, but the story of the great upheaval and the loss of a continent with its culture and knowledge was told to me several times, and always with great emphasis.

The road over the Serra d'Arrabida wanders on, with sea, land and sky as a perpetual picture, the ground on either side a mass of colour from the carpeting shrubs and flowers. The range of hills ends suddenly and the road hurries down their side with many twists and curves till it reaches Setubal.

Here we took a boat and our picnic lunch of fruit, local wine and fresh sardines, which the boatmen grilled for us over live charcoal. The sardines are surely a different fish from those we get in tins, and they are far more delicious.

The great bay of Setubal was empty but for a German tramp steamer flying the Swastika. I could not resist making the sign of the clenched fist to some of the crew who leant over her side watching us as we sailed past. This caused great consternation amongst our boatmen and to the kind Portuguese friend who was with us. Had they nurtured a viper unawares? A Communist! To make the sign alone was dreadful! I was much amused, for, as I assured them, there was no one who was more of a dyed-in-the-wool Conservative than I; but the sight of the flag and the faces under it made me think of the misery that had already come from Germany, and I told them that my clenched fist was a gesture of defiance, not at the crew but at the German Nazi mentality. I don't think I quite convinced them, for they continued to look at me for some time with questioning eyes.

Ahead of us the long point of Troia rose from the sea only a few feet above water-level, a mist of sand and low shrub. The skeleton of a ship lay in the small lagoon and a few fishermen's huts were all that remained of what had been, centuries ago, a large and prosperous town. Even the name Troia is of later date, for the earliest name by which it was known was Cetobriga. The ruins of the city may have been called Troia by learned professors in Renaissance days, when a statue was discovered there, Roman inscriptions and a temple of Jupiter

Ammon. More treasures were found after a great storm in 1814 which washed away some of the burying sand. The floods uncovered more ruins as well as a great lead casket full of beautiful silver candelabra and other things, which the savants of that day pronounced to be of Phœnician origin. Some excavations were made in 1850, which were of short duration. A fine Roman house was uncovered and many coins dug up, but funds soon ran out, and I do not know if the excavations were ever repeated. The town of Cetobriga must have flourished there for some time, and Setubal, across the bay, carries in its name a remembrance of the earlier town.

The coins discovered in 1850 tell of a rise from a small trading station in the reign of the Emperor Trajan to that of a city in the time of Theodosius. Was it destroyed by the Visigoths in the fifth century when they overran Spain and Portugal? It must have fallen suddenly, as no Roman money was found after that of Arcadius and Honorius, the Emperors of the East and West, sons of Theodosius.

Phœnician coins were also dug up there, as well as at Setubal, whose name may well be of Phœnician origin. Strabo and Avienus tell us of the trade by these great adventurers along the Atlantic and Mediterranean coast of Spain and Portugal. We know from Pliny that they had trading stations in Portugal and elsewhere.

They have left other traces of their passage besides coins and place-names. For here on the Portuguese coast you can still see the strange types of fishermen and women, with their finely cut features, large eyes and dark skins, in sharp contrast to the rounder faces and blunt features of the rest of the peasantry. There are also the fishing boats with the watchful eye painted on the prow—another Phœnician legacy.

Now Troia had little to show us. The shifting sands had covered the excavations of nearly a century ago. There were a few traces of walls where the sea had washed high against the sandbanks and uncovered them, but nothing else. The sandy shore was thick with a grey-green shrub covered with a mist of white pea-shaped blooms ; the air was heavy with their scent. The flora of Troia is different from that of the land facing it across the bay. For many years ballast from visiting ships had been dumped on to the point, and with it came many strange seeds which have grown and flourished, but it was too early to see them in flower—all but the lovely shrub, *Retama monosperma*, which I did not find elsewhere. I wish I knew more of the story of mysterious Troia ; under its sand must lie much history and perhaps many treasures. What was the cause of its decay and downfall ?

III

BLESSING THE COD-FISH FLEET

THE morning of 6th April was clear and bright, the air fresh and the intense blue of the sky dappled with white clouds. The far side of the Tagus was softened by a slight haze. The whole water-front, stretching from the docks to Belem, was alive. As I looked down from my window high up, I could see below me streams of people, all intent and quiet, and all going in one direction. The ships in the river were alive with flags and bunting, and the river itself a mass of busy small boats. It was the day of the Blessing—the Blessing of the Cod-Fish Fleet before their long journey and their many months in the perils of fog and sea off the Newfoundland banks.

Dried and salted cod-fish, *bacalhau*, is the staple food of the Portuguese peasant. All small grocery shops are festooned with the dry fish. Legend has it that the younger Albuquerque called his beautiful new palace at Azeitão " Bacalhoa " in grateful memory of the food which the hardy seamen lived on during their long voyage over the oceans of the world. It is part of Portuguese life. The ships are blessed every year just before they sail, by the cardinal, the papal nuncio or a bishop.

They had gathered in the river, each ship painted the colour of the private fleet to which she belonged, grey, dark red, striped. In the old days the ships were small and ill-found, and many did not return from the long voyage. Now they are large, many-masted schooners, with engine-power to help if the winds fail, and the men who sail in them are well looked after.

I hastily got my cameras and permit for the dock area and joined the crowd. There was a reverence in this multitude, bent on joining in a great communal prayer, yet they were gay and happy, and the air was full of laughter. The high spot of the morning was the procession of the cardinal's barge down the line of ships, ending at the flagship. The ships had been hives of industry for days. I had watched the boats dashing back and forth, bringing food, salt for the salting of the fish, water—and, once the supply was in, the great cleaning and polishing of everything. The sailors spit and polish ! That morning the whole river had burst into colour, and the ships themselves were hung with pennants, flags and bunting. Their sails were unfurled and hung flapping in the breeze as they swung at anchor—huge red, brown and white birds settled for a moment to rest. I did not know where best to go, and, above all, from where to photograph. A friendly policeman, overcome with curiosity at seeing a foreigner there, for the crowd was all Portuguese and it was very early, wandered towards me, passing back and forth several times, and finally summoned up his courage :

" Did the senhora want any help ? Had she a permit to photograph, and please, why two cameras ? Was not one enough ? "

I told him that the colours were so beautiful everywhere in Portugal I was taking coloured photographs as well as ordinary ones, so that I could see those colours again when I returned to a colder, grey country.

" Colour photographs," he said. " I have never heard of them. It would be a great thing to see one."

I asked if he would like one of himself.

" What ! The senhora would do that ? His fiancée lived in Coimbra in the north, and it would be a joy to send her such a wonder. It would help, when she looked at it, to pass the weary time till they had collected enough money and goods to marry on. Times were hard and it was slow work collecting. Still, if God wills, the time will pass, and a colour photograph would be a wonderful present to send her."

An interested crowd had by now collected, all wanting to know what we were talking about. He suddenly bethought himself of his dignity as an official, and demanded :

" Room for the good senhora. How in the name of the Saints could she photograph when so closely pressed about by the crowd ? Make room, there ! Could not they see that the senhora was a serious lady of importance ? Why, she had a permit to photograph everywhere, and with as many cameras as she could carry ! "

Soon I had posed him, while the crowd pressed behind him, shouting questions. They, too, wanted to see a coloured photograph. They really did not believe I could take one. I hope the policeman was not disappointed when I sent it to him.

Perhaps he expected a large coloured portrait, not a small transparency, bright though the colours were. While I posed him, I asked if it was the cardinal who blessed the fleet every year.

"Oh no, Senhora. It depends. One year the fleet had very bad luck. Several ships were lost and few fish were caught. Of course someone else had to bless it the next year. Some bishop did it, and it was most successful. But now it was different. Now we had our own beloved cardinal. He will surely bring all good blessing to the fleet. Why, he is the best cardinal of all the Papal College. The only fear in Portugal is that some day others may discover this too, and he might be taken from here and elected Pope. It would be a great honour for Portugal, but God forbid it, for we love and reverence our cardinal. May it be God's will that he spend many years with us. He is a very young man as cardinals go, Senhora, and no one knows the depth of his goodness and charity."

I had just finished and started to walk on when there was a sudden shout ; the Blessing had begun. Down the river came the cardinal's barge, followed by streams of others. All traffic ceased and a great quiet settled on the crowd. The barge passed slowly down the line of ships blessing each one as it passed by. The crews knelt on their decks to receive the blessing. On the shore one or two knelt, and as the barge came closer, like a wave the whole crowded mass fell to their knees, joining in the prayer for the fleet and the men before their long, perilous journey. At the end of the line of ships the barge turned. The crowd was on its feet again, laughing and talking. It broke up and turned towards home. The cardinal's barge came to the flagship of the fleet and stopped. There the prelate was to join other notables in a great banquet before she sailed. This was a strictly Portuguese affair.

The foreign diplomats watched from other ships, but were not invited to the feast. One by one the ships, with their gay flags still flying, slipped their anchors and were off. Nowadays they all have engines, so that although their sails were hoisted, they flapped and hung idly until caught by the Atlantic winds outside the bar. Then their sails filled and the ships heeled over, the water breaking on their bows as they gathered speed. Soon the sea was covered with their great sails rounding the

CODFISH FLEET

BASIN IN OLD KITCHEN AT MANIQUE

SANTO ANTONIO DA USSA

bend of Cabo da Roca one by one, like a flock of gulls on their way to the feeding-grounds. The flagship still tarried. At last the feast was over. The prelate's barge was by her side. Soon it turned up the river, followed by all the others of his company. The flagship's anchor was soon up, and she followed her fleet like a mother hen who has remained till her last chick has been safely shepherded on its way. The cod-fish fleet had sailed.

I often wonder why we do not eat the very good and nutritious *bacalhau*. For those adventurous souls who like to try something new from something old, I am giving a few recipes on how to cook it. The most important thing is the washing of the fish, and the quick disposal of the washing water, which smells the house out if it is not at once thrown away. The fish is delicious and can be cooked in many ways. There is a story of a peasant who suddenly made a large fortune after years of hard work, and asked all his rich new friends to dine. During his life he had been too busy to think of fancy food, but, of course, there was always *bacalhau*, so the great feast consisted of thirty different dishes—dishes of the fish—all different and all good.

RECIPES FOR PORTUGUESE "BACALHAU" (DRIED AND SALTED COD-FISH)

Bacalhau Blanket.—Soak the *bacalhau* for about thirty-six hours or more. Boil until it is sufficiently cooked, with an onion, and, when cooked, pound in a mortar till it is in shreds. Mix with seasoned mashed potatoes and serve hot in a mound garnished with parsley and hard-boiled eggs.

Bacalhau with White Sauce.—Boil *bacalhau* till cooked, then break into small pieces and sprinkle with grated nutmeg. Make a good white *béchamel* sauce, surround the fish with rice or mashed potatoes and cover with the sauce made hot. It is much improved if there is some white wine mixed in the last water in which the fish is soaked before cooking, or if some of the wine is sprinkled on it before covering with the white sauce.

Bacalhau Rico.—Soak the middle cut for three days, changing the water every day, and put it in salt and water. Before preparing, wash and dry it and rub it with a little garlic and salt. Take a deep fireproof dish and line the bottom with onions. Place the *bacalhau* on top of them, pepper it lightly, cover with

3

plenty of olive-oil and put in the oven and boil. Not even the bottom layer should turn brown. Serve in the same dish, first pouring off any surplus oil.

You can make excellent fish-cakes from *bacalhau*, and also a soufflé if it is well shredded and pounded in a mortar. In large flakes it is good for fritters. The side pieces, which are thin, are good for this. The important thing is to soak the fish well, changing the water several times.

IV

SANTO ANTONIO DA USSA

WE were sitting on the covered terrace at Bacalhoa watching the wind sweep up the distant Tagus from the Atlantic, tearing and pulling till it wearied and lost itself amongst the pines, oaks and fruit trees in the long, low country between us and the river.

While we sat, a friend told us of the many concealed and almost unknown places hidden amongst those trees. To the north, he had read, was an ancient chapel dedicated to St. Anthony and now lost to knowledge in the cork woods that stretched, a grey-green mist, towards the hills farther north across the river. Somewhere there was Jacome Ratton's farm and the chapel that he found ruined, and restored.

Jacome Ratton, Knight of the royal house of Portugal, Chevalier of the Order of Christ, ex-Merchant of the City of Lisbon, and Deputy to the Supreme Royal Tribunal of Commerce, Agriculture, Industry and Navigation, was a Frenchman who came to Portugal at the age of ten, and at the age of fourteen joined his parents in business, becoming a partner at seventeen. He remained in Portugal for over sixty years (May 1747–1810), for fifty of which he was a Portuguese subject, and by his foresight and industry created the large farm at Baroca d'Alva, and planted the great cork forests which are now all that remain of his property. He was imprisoned and finally deported in 1810 in the British frigate *Lavinia*, Lord William Stuart commanding.

The reason for his imprisonment and deportation was his extreme friendliness to the commanders and officers of the French invading armies during the Peninsular War.

Discussing the buying of the lands of Baroca d'Alva, he says in his book of memories and reflections written for the information of his beloved children :

" Having been brought up since the age of fourteen when I entered my father's firm as a merchant and a man of business, I am well versed in the many vicissitudes to which such enterprises expose those who take part in them. I, therefore, made up my mind that, to assure my family of always counting on a decent livelihood in this country, it would be a good plan to invest in farming, though I did not intend to give up my other business enterprises.

" Therefore, when at the beginning of the year 1767 I had occasion to visit the vast and deserted lands of Baroca d'Alva, I was greatly struck by the possibilities of same, especially having in mind the proximity to Lisbon and their easy access by water, seeing that the tides penetrated them along the Ribeira das Enguias. Though I then counted only thirty years of age and had no experience whatever of agricultural matters, I resolved to rent these great tracts of land for the sum of one thousand milreis per annum. Of this sum I was to retain two-fifths, in return for which I took on the obligation of repairing and adding to the irrigation canals, as was shown to be necessary, and carry out any other improvements which seemed indispensable. The improvements carried out were to be repaid to me when the contract came to an end.

" The lease was approved by the Crown, but as I foresaw that the settlement of the claims at the end of same would be of extreme difficulty, I asked for and obtained that no rent was to be paid during the first ten years of the lease, which would after that be transformed into a perpetual leasehold at half the previously arranged rent.

" The area of the lands in question is about one square league, of which about two-fifths are rich lowlands and three-fifths sandy agricultural lands, which, when I took over, were covered with brushwood, often swept by the most destructive fires. The lowlands were in their greater part nothing but swamps during each high tide.

" As for buildings, I found nothing but an ancient chapel next to a ruined house, where a poor goatherd used to take shelter. While opening the foundations for the farmhouse I wished to build on the spot, I found traces of pottery and glassware that confirmed the rumour that a glass works had once been established thereabouts.

" I also found in the valley known as Santo Antonio da Ussa, close to a small lake surrounded by willows, a small semi-ruined building built roughly in the shape of a pigeon-

cote, of about eighteen handbreadths (*palmos*) in diameter
and twenty to twenty-five in height, the roof being domed.
It was surrounded by a wall of crenellated construction something like a small fort. It was said to be of extremely ancient
construction, but its story had been lost. Inside I found
traces of an altar dedicated to St. Anthony, and tradition
had it that the image of this Saint had, many years previously,
been transferred to the other chapel of which I spoke above.

"I had the altar repaired, and gave instructions that Mass
was to be celebrated there on all Sundays and Holy days."

Our friend had not seen the chapel, though he knew the
country and thought that the farm was still in existence. Perhaps
the chapel might have survived too.

Early one morning three of us started out to see if we could
find it. Food we took in baskets, as we had no idea how long
the trip would take. To guide us we had maps and the few and
faint directions copied from Jacome Ratton's *Memoirs*.

After Setubal we turned north towards Montejo, through
thickly wooded and cultivated country that was low and sandy
in parts, with stone pines alternating with cork woods.
Flocks fed on the high roadside banks and fat sheep, the ewes
with udders large with milk to be shared between the hungry
lambs and the peasant owner, who makes a delicious cheese
from it. After Montejo we turned east, and were soon in lonely
country. The map showed few roads ; the one good road
leading towards Pegois was not for us. We had to find our
way to the cork woods and lowlands that Jacome Ratton wrote
of, farther north near the River of Eels (Ribeira das Enguias),
between it and the Tagus. In his days perhaps as now, the tides
came up to fill the ditches and turn the lowlands into swamp.
There were no villages, no farms and no traffic on the long road
that stretched before us. It seemed to go nowhere and was
without a sign of life, with only the sandy flats and cork oaks on
either side as far as we could see. We knew that we must be
somewhere near our goal—if it was where we thought—and we
stopped for the hundredth time to look at our instructions and
to wonder what to do, and whether it was best for us to go on.
Suddenly out of a lane there came, as if to rescue us, a rough-
coated stallion, ridden by a peasant carrying his small son

pillion behind him. The boy was wrapped in a Joseph's coat of many bright colours, banded with vivid green to match the long, pointed knitted cap which his father wore pulled well down on his head, the end dangling. He stopped quickly when he saw us, and looked at us with wonder. Such a car, a large Ford V8 station wagon, was a strange sight in those lonely parts—in fact, foreigners were a great curiosity, and almost unknown. As we questioned him, he hailed a hidden friend, telling him to come quickly and see what he had found wandering about the lanes, and asking, if you please, for, as far as he knew, a non-existent chapel of Santo Antonio, whose memory be blessed. We weren't really lost, he said ; if we were, this good and kindly Saint would surely find us—if we asked to be found. But that was not what we wanted. We wanted to find *him* or one of his many sanctuaries, and that was not so easy. Yes, the oak woods stretched for many leagues beyond the banks of the river ; there were no roads, and it was impossible for us to go farther except by the high road on which we were. Yes, there was a farm—a pig farm—far away, but the dykes cut it off, and our wagon would not fit the narrow lanes. Nothing daunted, we finally got some directions from him which he gave with great reluctance—he might have been sending us into dangerous and bandit-infested country from his looks and asides to his friend. On our own heads be it if we were lost in the forest ; he had done *his* best to stop us.

At last, following these vague directions, we came to a lovely shrine at Alatas, set seemingly without reason in a large empty place, a few farm buildings at its edge. Then the questioning began again, to be greeted with the same wondering doubt. We were despairing and almost ready to turn home defeated, when a newcomer announced that *he* knew of a chapel—yes, a very old one. Rumour had it that it was originally a Moorish fort, which guarded the edge of the land where the waters of the river came at high tide to cover much of what is now dry and culti-vated land, but, Senhora, it is impossible for you to get there ; there are no roads—in the cork woods one is easily lost—there are no landmarks and, except for those who know, the place is a maze. And so it proved to be. The track we finally took left the road full of purpose and very definite as to where it was to go and how, but it soon tired, wandered, lost interest and turned in circles : this we realized when a pool overshadowed by a solitary stone pine, which we had passed and photographed half an hour sooner, loomed up again. Little grew under the trees but the many-coloured *Cistus*, and patches of a small tulip with yellow-pointed petals and a band of red up the centre of each (*Tulipa australis*). The ground they grew in was as hard as rocks, and it took me a long time to hack out a bulb.

At last, tired and almost despairing of finding our chapel, we turned down a very faint track. It was our last and only chance. Good St. Anthony must have been with us, for suddenly we were looking across a deep water-filled dyke at some lone farm buildings. From the noise and smell we knew we were at the pig farm which Jacome Ratton had built there over a hundred and sixty years before. The pigs were strange-looking creatures, with thin, long, razor-sharp backs, which curved down as if the weight of their bodies was too much for their weak spines. Their noses turned up sharply and their eyes were covered by big, heavy ears. Many were a rich golden brown with a glint of red ; some were spotted.

There was only one way over the dyke and that was by a wobbly bridge, but the brave Ford took it and we were soon in the farmyard, with a curious, surging mass of pigs nosing at us. At the noise they made, a swineherd appeared to see what the fuss was about, and seemed even more surprised than the pigs. A shout brought two other farm-hands to look at the strangers and to speculate about them. The same questions were quickly answered this time. Why, yes—yes, of course there was the Chapel of Santo Antonio da Ussa, but far into the woods, and now surrounded by the lake on whose shores it had been in Jacome Ratton's time. Impossible to get there unless we walked for miles ; that—pointing to the Ford—would never make it. Why, it was too wide to pass between the trees. Besides, we would surely be lost ; there were no roads and no landmarks. The sight of a note quickly changed the possibilities. Perhaps if the senhoras didn't mind very rough country—yes, Pedro would go with us ; he had to see about an errant sow who preferred to farrow far from home and who was still unfound. This would be a chance to look for her.

Into the woods we plunged again, and this time there was no track. We followed a low wall for some way, branched off

to the left, scraped through the narrow paths between the oaks—
and everywhere were the strange-looking pigs. Pedro told us
that they were supposed to be the descendants of some brought
from China centuries ago in merchant ships for food on the long
voyage. Some had survived and lived to start a race in this new
country.

Through the trees came a glint of water, and suddenly the
lake, island and chapel were before us. The separation from
the main forest must have been recent, for the water at one point
was very narrow and not very deep, but just too much so for us
to ford it. The island was tiny. There was hardly room for
the chapel with its walls and attendant stone pines. Two large
trees guarded it on either side, and their children were growing
strongly on the small remaining ground. The round tower of
the chapel, with its pointed tiled roof, was surrounded by a low
crenellated wall. The entrance to the tower was of much later
date than the rest, for it was a baroque-type doorway with a
plain door. The round tower was obviously Moorish and so
were the walls. As far as we could see, both were of plaster-
covered stone. The pointed roof was also later in date, perhaps
eighteenth century, and made of dark tiles. There was some
small roofless building attached to the wall and tower.

The sinking sun touched the chapel with a golden light,
throwing the shadows towards us across the narrow water. It
had a strange aloofness, withdrawing itself, as if, after years of
usage, neglect and forgetfulness, it had encircled itself with water
and now waited in quiet and peace for the final crumbling.
It did not want to be found. The willows Jacome Ratton had
written of were gone. In their place a few old oaks with twisted
stems leaned towards the tower—its ancient guardians, now too
old to protect it. I felt sorry that we had intruded on its lonely
privacy. Looking back, I wish I had not told others where it
was, though the difficulty of getting there would prevent most
people from going. It did not want to be seen, and as we left,
it settled down again with a sigh, to the peace and quiet of death.

Pedro told us that no one went there now—in fact, hardly
anyone knew of it. How did we strangers come there when
people a few leagues away were not aware of its existence? He
looked at us with perplexity and curiosity, but the charming
friendliness of the Portuguese overcame his suspicion. *His*

pleasure was to have given us pleasure, and now his wish and duty was to leave us and to find the lost sow, who was surely not far away. She would not be, as dykes cut the woods and pigs did not like their steep sides nor the water at the bottom.

Going back was as difficult as retracing one's steps through a maze. We could follow our own tracks sometimes when the ground was fairly soft, so each landmark was eagerly looked for. We made few mistakes and soon we were back at the farm, where another kind swineherd led us over rickety bridges and through fields by a short-cut to the main road. Back in Lisbon no one had heard of our chapel, and many people doubted its existence, till my photographs proved that somewhere and somehow we had stumbled on a tiny bit of forgotten history.

V

PROCESSIONS AND WITCHES

ONE of Portugal's greatest charms is the intense religious feeling of the simple people and their belief in all supernatural things.

There are processions and blessings for all things and at all times. Some of these follow the seasons of ancient pagan festivals, and in many parts there are still relics of pagan beliefs and witch-cults which mingle with their Christian traditions. They are still very much a part of their lives. Some of these rites deal with the normal changes of the seasons, others with the fertility of crops. In the Douro country the carved figure of a woman is buried in the corn after it is thrashed; and in the same country, when the harvest is gathered, a pole is erected on the top of which are flowers, and above them are placed two small figures. These are removed by the youths, who quickly rush with them towards the nearest house, pursued by the local maidens who try to catch them and get the dolls before they can enter. I cannot tell what this ceremony means.

As a protection against witches, bunches of herbs, rosemary, broom and, in some places, small crosses are put at the four corners of a ploughed field on 1st May. There is also a rope across the entrance to a village on the same date. Stretched high, it is hung with garlands of flowers and the same herbs, which are kept throughout the year as a symbol of fertility. As a protection, on 1st May all openings in the house, including the chimneys, through which a witch could pass, are filled with sprigs of broom, and in the cow-houses are hung more garlands.

There is a charming legend about broom which brings the use of it from the pagan into the Christian orbit.

As Christ and the disciples sat at the Last Supper a branch of broom was placed in the window of His house—a signal to those who wished to capture Him—but when they came, every window and door in the village was ablaze with the yellow flower.

The story of the moss-rose is another of the many which link flowers of all kinds with the life of Christ.

The weary Child wandered asking for shelter from the noonday heat. The proud and stately trees refused to lower their branches to give Him shade, but a humble rose-bush said, " Creep under here. I will spread myself over You and You can rest." When the cool of the evening woke the Child, He came forth from His lowly sleeping-place. Touching the rose, He told it that never again would it have thorns ; moss would grow in their place. It had become the Rose of Christ.

In telling these stories I cannot lay claim to any knowledge of folklore, but only a great interest in the subject. Those who

want more details, well studied and presented, should read Rodney Gallop's extremely interesting book on Portugal, where all the various cults and rites are fully described. I am only relating the things I saw personally or was told by the most reliable witnesses, and by friends of mine.

The sun was hot and we were tired. Digging for Roman remains sounds romantic, but if it is not very successful, it can be merely tiresome. Marion had hoped to find a tessellated pavement, for one had been uncovered near where we were, but the only result of our labour was a large plain flooring tile, like those still in use in many parts of Portugal. Below us in the small quarry a workman watched with deep interest, quickly returning to his work when he saw that we had noticed him. At last, hot and bored at our lack of success, we stopped and sat down in the shade of the quarry-side.

" Would you like some tea ? " Marion asked the quarry-man.

" Thank you, gracious Senhora. It would be an honour," he answered, and came over to take the cup we offered.

He went off to drink it out of sight, as it would not have been polite to do so in our presence. When he returned, after a few minutes he ventured to say :

" The senhoras were not successful—no, of course not. The treasure they were doubtless after was too well bewitched and could not be found by just digging. Why, it was well and truly guarded by a very powerful enchanted Mooress, as was well known, and could only be discovered if she wished it, or if they performed the necessary rites to free it from enchantment, which God forbid."

It was no use telling him that it was not treasure we were after, but traces of ancient history.

" Tell us about the Mooress," we asked. " Is she then so well known, and have you seen her ? "

" Well known, yes, Senhora ; she has guarded the treasure from time beyond count. No, I have never seen her. She is not as modern as that, but my father saw her and never forgot it, nor ceases to tell us of it and to warn us against digging where she guards."

" What was she like ? " we asked. " What did your father see ? "

" Senhora, he was returning from a visit to some friends late in the evening many years ago, and as he approached the place where we know that the treasure is hidden, he heard the whistling snakes, but did not see them. A little farther on, the Mooress suddenly sprang out at him. She was tall, in the shape of a woman, but covered with long brown hair. My father ran as fast as he could, not waiting to see or hear more, and warned us of the danger. None of us have ever seen her, but I have both seen and heard the snakes. Late one night I passed near by, carefully watching in case the Mooress should jump out at me. Suddenly I heard a loud whistle, and there, Senhora, on that very stone, under those trees were the whistling snakes."

" What were they like ? " we asked.

" Snakes, just snakes, but they were covered with long hairs. They whistled at me so loudly that I took to my heels and have never passed by here at night since that day. I pray you ladies to be careful what you do, trying to rifle the treasure. It can do you no good, and will not be found until someone is brave enough, and wicked enough, to use the rites St. Cyprian writes of in his book on the Evil One. Bewitched and hidden treasure can only be found by using the Unholy Mass which he describes."

We assured him that we were not looking for treasure, but only for history, and as we had not been successful, we would not go on with our digging. His relief was great, and we left him to his quarrying and took our tile home.

The legend of this treasure was so universal that several peasants near my friend's home felt that they would risk the sin of the Unholy Mass necessary to raise the Devil. The story was told by Joaquim who took part in it.

" It was a dark night, Senhora, when we started for Monte Crasto. Each of us had our staves. One carried a lantern, another the evil book. The hill when we got to it was dark and thickly covered with pine woods. Near where the treasure is hidden and bewitched we inscribed the seal of Solomon (pentacle) and stood within its magic protection. The first sign that the spell was breaking was a great buzzing swarm of flies which surrounded us. We knew then that the Devil was not far off. Suddenly he appeared outside our circle in the shape of a fox. One careless man had allowed the end of his stave to protrude beyond the seal. The Devil got it and started belabouring us, for we were no longer protected. In the fray the lantern was knocked over, and no one knew who was his assailant. When it finally stopped, we were all badly beaten and one poor fellow lay near to death. The fear of God came upon us, for we realized what we had done. To save his soul and ours, we carried him to the priest and there confessed our sins. The penance put upon us was to carry him to the chapel on the top of another hill. It was in vain to save his life. God will that his soul be saved."

· The staves the men carried are made of quince wood. They are big and are used for many purposes. If one is dropped on the horns of the draft oxen, it shows them which way to turn. The small goad at one end is used to encourage them if they slacken their pace. It serves as a stick on which to rest while watching cattle grazing, and as a walking-stick. These staves are good weapons in a fight, and can do great damage.

The belief in werewolves is widespread, as Rodney Gallop shows in his interesting book. I never came across it personally, but a friend told me that she had questioned her maid.

" Do you know of any werewolves, Maria, or have you heard of any ? "

" Why, certainly, Senhora. They are well known, and even here in the village there has been one, and in such a respectable family. It caused them much trouble. You know, Senhora, that if and when you discover who is a werewolf, the only cure is to watch it on the nights it goes out (some say Wednesdays and Saturdays). It goes to the tallest tree in the neighbourhood and leaves its clothes. These are easy to find if the werewolf is an animal like a wolf, a cat or a hare, but if it is a bird, it is far more difficult, for then the clothes are on the topmost branches instead of lying at the foot of the tree. These clothes must be collected, taken away and burned. The werewolf then returns to normal and does not wander again. You know the one in this village, Senhora ; she is the chemist's daughter ! And has been the cause of much sorrow to her family till she was cured."

" How did they discover it, and how did it happen that she became such a thing ? " asked my friend.

" The family noticed that on certain days their daughter was greatly exhausted, and when blisters and callouses were discovered on her hands there was no doubt as to what she was. As usual, she was the seventh child. Sometimes it happens that a person is bewitched, but far more often it comes naturally to the seventh child."

The belief in witches is deeply ingrained in the Portuguese. Peasants and servants will go to the doctor as an extra precaution, but they seldom take his medicine. The witches' potions are far more popular. The cook of another friend of mine complained of continual indigestion, and was finally persuaded to see the doctor, who told her she ate far too much and too quickly. All went well for a short time, till one day the doctor was sent for. The cook was in agony. His medicine had caused it, she said. When he examined her he found a broken rib.

" How did this happen ? " he demanded. " You did not have this before. Have you been to the witch ? "

" Oh yes, Senhor Doctor, I have."

" What happened ? "

" After giving me some herbs she made me lie on the floor, and while whispering her incantations she jumped over me, but the Devil caught her foot and she fell." (The cook was very fat and the witch was old.) " Since then I have had this terrible pain."

" Well," scolded the doctor, " she broke your rib, and that comes from going to a witch and not doing as I told you. Ask her to cure you now that she has hurt you ! "

Planting done by the phases of the moon is a very widespread practice in many countries. In Portugal they say, however, that potatoes lifted at any time but during the waning moon will not keep, and hens are put to sit at the waxing moon, otherwise the eggs will be infertile.

These relics of an ancient past mingle with the intense belief in the active personal power of the Saints and images, in honour of whom various processions take place. So strong is this belief in the Saints that they are not only asked to pray and help, but are threatened that if they do not succeed in their intercession, dire punishment will be meted out to them by their supplicants.

Many sacred figures are found all over the country, each with its own history and its special fête day, and they are the very special pride and property of the village and district to which they belong. In some places the image is so powerful in its virtue that many surrounding villages and towns claim a share in it. Nossa Senhora do Cabo at Espichel is the precious possession of fifty parishes. She spends a year in each of her fifty shrines, and every fiftieth year she starts her pilgrimage again, with Cintra as her first stop.

At Espichel itself the church stands at the end of a long point. Leading to it is a broad grassway, bordered on either side by rows of small houses—one for each parish of Nossa Senhora's pilgrimage. In the old days pilgrims came there, sure of finding shelter in the house of their parish. Now many are in ruins, but a few are lived in permanently.

The great days are over when the multitudes set out on

foot to take Our Lady to her next resting-place, or to make a pilgrimage to her. Then, if night overtook the pilgrims, the great houses on the road opened their doors, and they were sheltered and fed. These houses always had large empty rooms kept free for this purpose.

Each village south of the Tagus sent, and still sends pilgrimages to the church at Espichel in memory of the great earthquake in 1755, and each village has its own day. Now the charity of hospitality is no more, for modern transport has changed the whole aspect of the pilgrimages. There is no time to walk nowadays. The charity of giving is still practised. I saw in Lisbon, Setubal, Azeitão and elsewhere crowds of poor, halt, maimed and old who clustered round the gates of houses where they received alms of food and bread on certain days of the week. " In Christ's name take this and begone." " A long life and health to you if God wills."

At Easter we watched the Host carried in procession through the courtyard and garden at Bacalhoa. The priest was preceded by men and boys in scarlet robes, carrying long white staves. Between the double rows of men walked small boys and girls. Their heads were crowned with flowers and wings of gauze lay on their shoulders. Then came the daughters of Mary in pale blue blouses, and in front of them walked a double row of girls in white, wearing red caps. A further guard of the red-robed men held their white staves like wands, and then followed the Host carried by the priest under a canopy, upheld at each corner by red-clad men, and at the side others carrying large lanterns on poles. The whole road from the church, to the court-yard, through the garden and back to the church, was thickly strewn with wild rosemary and lavender. The road was bordered by a reverent crowd, who knelt to receive the blessing as the Host passed. This the priest held high, and turned from side to side so that all should share its virtues. As the procession passed, the people rose from their knees, each one taking a spray of the rosemary to keep, as one does the blessed palms on Palm Sunday, and they joined in the procession till they reached the church, where the doors were flung open and they all poured in for the High Mass.

At Nazaré on the Festa do Senhor dos Passos do Nazaré, the twisting road that runs from the fishing village on the shore to the church and shrine on the high cliff was packed with a slowly moving procession, a vivid representation of the Passion and Death of Our Lord. Carved figures in the stations of the Cross were carried on carts. The sepulchre had a most lifelike body of Christ lying in it. The weeping Mother and disciples followed, and everywhere there were tiny children dressed as St. John, the Christ Child, the Virgin Mary and various Saints. The whole village and neighbourhood followed and so great was the crowd that only a small portion of it could get into the church.

I stole away to the shrine of Our Lady of Nazaré, a tiny chapel hanging on the cliffside, overlooking the sandy sweep of the great bay below. It is in two portions, with the small altar above, and down rough steps the actual shrine of Our Lady. Below her is the iron-bound box in which she was found after having been lost for many years. One legend about her says that the saintly Dom Fuas Roupinho, governor of the district, so angered the Devil by his goodness that in order to lure him to his doom, the Devil changed himself into a deer and, dashing to the cliffside, leapt over. Dom Fuas Roupinho followed in his enthusiasm, but Our Lady upheld him and his horse as they leapt, and brought them safely to ground. The hoof-mark of his horse is still to be seen on the cliffside. The tiny place was a blaze of light from the masses of votive candles left by the men, women and children, each come to ask a boon, a blessing, or to say a prayer of thankfulness. There was a steady stream of quiet, reverent worshippers as I knelt near the altar.

There is the Feast of Our Lady of Nazaré, which lasts from 8th to 15th September, when the countryside is *en fête* and the village is crowded with holiday-makers, and when there are games, bull-fights and local tournaments, in sharp contrast to the sadness and quiet of the Easter procession.

Janas, a very little-known village in the plain beyond Cintra, is the scene of quite a different pilgrimage. Here, on 17th August, the farmers bring their cattle to be blessed by the good St. Mamede. His little chapel is round, with a pointed tiled roof. The walls are dead white, and part of the circumference is an open veranda. The roof covers it, and there is a low wall at the base from which this is upheld by pillars. The chapel is believed to have been built on the site of a far more ancient

4

building, a pagan temple, for a very early inscription on a stone was found near by. The festival held in the honour of St. Mamede is doubtless also the relic of ancient pagan worship.

The cult of St. Mamede was brought to Portugal by the many poor noblemen who, inspired by the success of a French knight, Henry of Burgundy, followed him to try and carve out estates for themselves at the expense of the Moors. St. Mamas, as he was known in France, lived in the third century A.D. He was born in Cappadocia, where a wave of persecution broke out under the Emperor Aurelian. His father, Theodotus, was executed, but they spared his mother, Rufina, as she was expecting a child. She afterwards died or was executed, for legend has it that Mamas was educated by a patrician matron. He taught Christianity to his fellow-pupils, and was arrested when he was twelve years old and brought before the Provincial Governor. Claiming his right as a Roman citizen, he appealed to Cæsar. When his case was brought before the Emperor's Court, every effort was made to break the boy's faith. He was tortured, stoned and thrown into the sea, but he escaped and took refuge in the desert, where he built himself a hermitage and made friends with the animals. The fame of his virtue attracted people from all over Cappadocia, who came to listen to him. Mamas was again arrested and tried for sorcery, tortured, condemned and thrown to the lions. The lions were apparently friends of his, for they would not injure him. When the Governor saw that he was still alive, he ordered him to be stoned and stabbed with a lance, and he died on 17th August, A.D. 293 at the age of fifteen.

Cappadocia afterwards became a great centre of Christianity and produced the Saints, Gregory and Basil. St. Gregory spoke of the great devotion to St. Mamas and the extraordinary number of pilgrims that came to venerate his relics. These were brought to Jerusalem and Constantinople. When the Christians of the East were obliged to send their sacred relics westwards before the advancing hordes of the Mussulmans, some went to France, where the devotion to St. Mamas became popular. Forty years before the First Crusade an arm of St. Mamas was sent to France from the Imperial Chapel in Constantinople. The rich jewels of this relic helped to finance the Second Crusade. After the Fourth Crusade the head of St. Mamas, with the original circlet of silver and its inscription, was awarded by the Papal Legate to the Bishop Gualem de Dampierre, who took it to his cathedral at Langres. In Portugal the cult grew, and St. Mamede, as he is called there, is looked upon as the patron saint of animals. At Janas, where his festival is held, the cattle are driven three times anti-clockwise round the chapel. If some can be persuaded to let their heads rest through the opening of the porch, they are indeed lucky and receive a special blessing. After the blessing is over, the priest receives offerings of wheat and bread, which are distributed among the poor. The chapel is full of offerings. Small images of wax, an arm, a leg, a breast, a sheep, a cow, chickens, dogs, a baby, are left as outward signs of blessings received.

The form of the chapel at Janas seems a very common one in mediæval Portugal. There is one near Palmella dedicated to São Gonçalo, where, before the Crusades or battles with the Moors in Portugal, the knights went on horseback and were blessed, the horses standing with their heads through the opening in the chapel. Portugal was an extremely useful training-ground for budding Crusaders. Many stopped off on the way to the East to help the Portuguese to free themselves from the Moors, and some went no farther. The land of milk and honey of the Romans proved too attractive. They were not always an unmixed blessing to the Christian inhabitants of the country, who would often have gone without their help. This was inclined to turn into " help themselves " in some cases, though others did good work.

There are many other festivals and processions. The most modern is at Fatima, where Our Lady appeared several times to some children. So much has been written of the wonderful miracles that have taken place there, and of the great pilgrimages to Fatima, that I am not attempting to add anything, nor can I write of other processions which I did not see. There is an interesting field of research for anyone who has the time to study these feasts and their origin.

VI

" MERCADOS " OR MARKETS

In the town the daily *mercado* is the meeting-place of the local housewives and servants—the conventional continental market.

In Lisbon there is an unusual one where only the fish that comes in half alive from the Atlantic fishing boats is sold. Huge eels, fresh sardines, red and grey mullet and many others lie in shimmering piles, which are quickly sorted and handed over to the many fish-women, who carry them away in large round baskets on their heads.

These women, who are called *varinas*, are one of the sights of Lisbon as they stride barefooted through the streets crying their wares. By law they are supposed to wear shoes, at least in the town, but I never saw them do so ; the shoes always hung from their arms or from the baskets on their heads. They are a race and community apart, and are supposed to be of Phœnician descent. They come from Povoa and Ovar as well as from other fishing villages along the coast. Those from Povoa particularly have preserved many ancient customs. All their possessions and fishing boats are stamped with the family mark —amongst these there are many Phœnician and early Greek symbols. They seldom if ever marry with the surrounding peasantry, and their property passes from father to younger son. It seems, from the researches made by Senhor Santos Graça, that the Póveiros are the purest in descent and have kept more strictly to the old customs. They are a blend of the original inhabitants with the Phœnicians, and there are small traces of Teutonic and Norman blood. They are a fine, upstanding race with good features.

The real markets or *feiras*, which are the meeting-place of the countryside, take place in small towns or large villages at regular intervals, sometimes every fortnight, sometimes every month. The villages are often called after the *feiras*, such as, Fiera dos Noves or Feira do Vinte tres—" Fair of the 9th " or " Fair of the 23rd." These sometimes function once a week for the local people, but the monthly fair is where the whole neighbourhood meets. The peasants come from great distances to them, walking often for four or five hours to get there. In the hill country, on the morning of the fair, you can see the long lines of people following the short-cuts over hill or dale, coming to the meeting-place with their merchandise. The women have white handkerchiefs over their heads and perhaps a small hat on top. They bring anything that can be carried, dead or alive, in baskets perched above their hat on a ring of rags— chickens, rabbits, eggs, fruit and corn. Their balance is so perfect that their baskets never fall—the women often knit as they walk, with a swinging gait, over the rough ground, their heads and shoulders motionless, all movement from the hips. The men carry nothing ; it is beneath their dignity to do so, but they lead cattle and sheep or drive pigs with a string tied to their legs.

Everything that a peasant wants can be bought at these fairs—cooking pots (pottery), baskets, rag rugs, which are often used as blankets, blankets made in the mountains from local wool, flour, beans, salt, rice, oil and eggs. There is no butter, for olive-oil is the fat used in its place. There is seldom tea or coffee. The usual diet of these hardy country folk is :

Breakfast.—Wine, which can be bought for less than a penny a bottle, made by most peasants for their own consumption, thin and sour but very refreshing and not very strong, and maize bread, with perhaps a piece of garlic. White bread is seldom eaten except by black-coated workers or town dwellers.

Midday.—A big bowl of very thick vegetable soup, often

made with beans and always olive-oil added for fat, more maize bread, dried salted cod (*bacalhau*), salted sardines or pickled pork. This pork is salted dry and kept in great chests. It is sometimes smoked as well.

Supper.—Supper is the same as breakfast. There are no sweets but fruits, if they have their own fruit trees, and no tea or coffee unless in towns, for no peasant wishes to walk ten or twelve miles to buy these when local wine is to be had.

At the fair everything is kept in separate sections, rows upon rows of pottery, pots of all shapes and sizes in hundreds, as well as the miniature pottery for children and pottery toys, which are all the toys they have. These are pottery bulls, strongly reminiscent of Minoan culture, orange or sometimes red men on horseback, whistles in the shape of birds, cocks, hens and pigeons, but none of the water whistles found in country fairs in the south of France. There are money-boxes in various shapes, also black pigs and hedgehogs covered with holes for tooth-picks. Here are rows of *pots de chambre* all decorated with free-hand designs of flowers, and some in miniature with affectionate motives round the rim, to be used as ash-trays.

I found the pottery stalls most delightful. There were earthenware bowls glazed inside in yellow, splashed with green, dishes white and green, others yellow with designs etched on them in coloured lines, a big fish, a flower, a cabbage. There were tiny teapots and cups of jaspé ware, dark green and blue, for a few pence. The yellow and green bowls cost twopence each, and are ideal for salad. The large dishes with etched designs are fireproof, and fish or meat baked in them is particularly good. Near Oporto I got some small red dishes decorated with a crude design in white. They are for baking individual portions of meat, and are supposed to give it a particular flavour, which I think they do, as well as keeping it very hot. The meat tasted like that grilled over a charcoal fire.

Caldas da Rainha is the great centre for a very ornate and special type of pottery found nowhere else. It is very brightly coloured green and yellow with a high glaze. There are dishes like big cabbage leaves, others flat like giant bay leaves—the same in small for butter-plates. There are yellow pumpkins, realistic oranges and lemons for jam-jars, as well as tea and coffee sets of various design. There is a fresh cleanness about this pottery which makes it charming for country houses. It is delightful, and is so cheap one can afford the risk of a few breakages on the way home. I have had various pieces in continual use for five years and they still keep their fresh bright glaze and colour.

In other places a highly glazed black pottery is made, such as at Estremoz, but I did not like the designs as much as the coloured ware. We were told that the huge water-jars came from Alcacer-do-Sol. I had seen them standing outside houses filled with water. The slight evaporation through their porous skin leaves the water icy cold on the hottest day. We went hunting for these jars several times, but never found the really large ones. Like the White Queen's jam, it was yesterday or to-morrow, but never to-day.

Other charming products which we found in some of the markets were the straw rugs and mats. They are woven in colours, thin and easily folded, and are perfect for the garden. Thick round cushions of woven grass could be found everywhere. They are for the olive presses. The olives are pressed between them and the oil filters through, leaving stones and skins behind. I find them good as garden cushions, on the grass or on stone seats.

Baskets, too, were another temptation. They were of every shape and size, some white, others made of the same coloured straw as the mats.

At every market was the second-hand stall where anything from broken keys to incense burners could be bought. Sometimes a treasure turns up, and everything is always wonderfully cheap.

At these markets the young men and girls went about in groups, all girls, all men, seldom mingling, but laughing when they met and shouting sallies at each other as they passed. The elders stood watching and gossiping. Some old women, surrounded by piles of flat loaves, with their unbrellas up against the sun, had their heads together listening, from their expression, to what seemed to be an interesting tale. Others saw to the weighing of their purchases in primitive scales, like those of blind justice. A mother tried on her small girl hat after hat, all exactly alike. The child paid no attention to what she was doing, but watched all around her with sharp, questioning eyes. Groups of girls showed each other what they had bought, some of which caused much laughter and backchat. There seemed no great anxiety to sell, but great politeness when anyone stopped to look and admire. No one was importuned to buy.

The clothes for sale at these markets were not very interesting though each district had some speciality of its own. The traditional dress of the country is dying out by degrees, and only certain things survive.

At Nazaré, where the fishermen wear blouses or jumpers with large checks and lines, you can get the material, of fine wool, in many patterns and colours. Near the bull-breeding country you find the white stockings, short coloured trunks and bright knitted caps that the *campinos* wear. The stockings are made of thick wool and have turnovers with a pattern of many colours.

At and near Viseu the market stalls and shops have enchanting hats, which I could not get farther south. The most popular shape was like a Chinese coolie hat, a flat plate with bright flowers and designs cut out of felt and pressed flat on to the straw, which was yellow, cream and sometimes other colours. They cost very little, and are most becoming and useful.

These markets are quite apart from the great fairs which are held after a religious festival, such as the Feast of St. Mamede at Janus or Nazaré, which only take place once a year. Then there are games, shooting and sports, but I never saw one of these fairs myself. In the markets cattle and live stock have their own separate section—cows, pigs, chickens, rabbits—away from the household goods and food. The donkeys at Cintra had a meeting-place of their own while their owners wandered round the market. The donkeys clustered near the central fountain, where they could drink when they wanted to and where they seemed to have a special parliament as they rubbed noses, with an occasional bray when their feelings needed a louder expression.

We were too early that year for the fruit, excepting oranges and lemons. Later there would be the delicious green melon which, when served in restaurants, is cut into long points so that you have more than half the melon to yourself. The grapes and figs are delicious ; the muscatels are so sweet they are almost like raisins. Later too, pineapples come from the Azores, and no one who has not eaten one of these can know what a pine-

FOUNTAIN AT ARRAIOLOS

FOUNTAIN AT MONTEMOR

apple really is. It is quite a different fruit from the kind we buy in England, full of juice, and the flesh is almost soft.

In Lisbon there is the weekly rag market. Here no food or live stock is sold. Nothing but household goods, furniture, clothes and the second-hand stalls with their piles of bits and pieces. I found there a set of twenty-four Chinese engraved mother-of-pearl knife and fork handles with silver caps, and with them one fork and knife still attached to the handles. It was not until cleaned by José at the Legation that I found the caps and fork were of eighteenth-century silver. I had them copied by a local silversmith, so the set is complete. The original cost was under £1, and the whole set when finished came to less than £5. Another time I found a lovely Cosway drawing in a very ornate baroque carved wooden frame. One wonders how it got there. There were many visits to this and other markets which yielded nothing but the joy of their colour and life.

VII

BULLS AND BULL-FIGHTS

In Portugal there are bull-fights called *teuradas*, fascinating displays of horsemanship, wonderful horses trained for the show-ring, each movement stylized by centuries of usage, beautiful clothes, bright colours and—the bull. His fierceness is untamed, but his horns are carefully padded, so that he can hurt no one in his mad rushes. He chases the horses, and their riders' pride is to let him come just so near and then to evade him. The greatest blot on their performance is a mark from the padded horns, which are supposed to be chalked, so that a touch shows on the horse's flank, to the great shame of the rider. As the bull charges, the rider flies before him, turning suddenly to place the long barbed *banderillos* in his neck, when the long paper streamers hang down ; a miss is greeted with groans, and a hit with shouts of delight by the crowd. At the end of the fight the bull has many of these streamers hanging from his neck.

When several of the riders have had their sport and shown off their skill and horsemanship, the bull is faced by a long line of men—the *furcados*—dressed in bright colours, green, red and white, with short trousers and round broad-brimmed hats. As the bull charges them, the first man seizes his horns, leaping on to his back with an action which reminded me of the Cretan bull-fighters shown on the bronzes and drawings of ancient Cretan art. The rest of the men close in, and after a brief struggle the bull is thrown on to his side, while the men seem to be in a mixed pile on top of him. Sometimes the first man misses his cue and the rest scatter quickly, to reform their lines elsewhere when they have drawn the bull's attention to themselves. When he has been thrown, the men bow low to the audience, now wild with excitement, fly to the sides and leap over the barrier. The bull gets to his feet, snorting with fury. He looks around the arena for someone to attack ; as he stands there, a picture of frustrated rage, the gates of the barrier open and in come the bell cows, trotting serenely and quietly. They scatter, and in a few minutes go out again by the gate. In their midst walks the tired and pacified bull, changed in one moment from a picture of fury into a quiet and gentle creature by his peaceful harem.

The riders in the contest of skill are dressed in beautiful eighteenth-century clothes, with lace jabots at their necks and long lace frills over their hands. The horses are stallions which have had years of training, and they are often more renowned than their riders. The bulls are of the same fierce and agile race used in Spain, where they fight to the death, not just for beauty and for art as they do in Portugal. Here the art of the rider and his horse is pitted against the quickness and cunning of the bull.

One of the largest breeders promised to show me the bulls in their wild breeding-grounds and how they are rounded up. We went north up the side of the Tagus, through Povas till we came to Villa Franca, beyond which was the Palha Blanco Quinta, belonging to our host, who had some of the best bulls in Portugal. The house overlooked the low, flat country lying towards the river. Behind us the hills were covered with trees and vines. On one hill was a tiny village crowned with a white-domed Moorish tower. Our host's house stood in a grove of orange trees. Near it was his private bull-ring, in which the bulls are tested for courage and quickness before they are sent out. Here budding bull-fighters can learn a little of their intricate profession, and some of the many ways to ride and to meet the bull.

We had our lunch under an arbour of bougainvillea, with arum lilies and geraniums in long borders by the paths which crossed the orange orchard. The maids who served us wore peasant dresses of blue, red and white, their heads tied in red handkerchiefs with long ends which fell on either side of their faces. They busily ran back and forth to the house, bringing out the delicious Portuguese food. Fish of all sorts we had, lobster, crabs, prawns in various sauces, and the rare and delicious sparkling Busaco wine, like mild champagne. Above us, on the roof of the house, stood the storks. Some were building their nests of twigs and small branches, others were already sitting. On each chimney was a complete family, though I thought I saw one father stork taking care of more than one nest. He certainly was very polite to two ladies alternately, dancing up and down and making a clacking sound, with his beak I think. The ladies took no notice of him, and they all treated the place as their own.

We were to go after lunch to see the rounding up of the bulls and perhaps the finest the ranch had produced for many years, one which was to be the prize bull for the fight in Madrid, the first to be held after the Civil War.

The ranch and its huge ranges was on the other side of the river. There was no bridge, only the very primitive ferry to take us across. The cars were run on to a narrow boat, hardly wide enough to take them. A block of wood under their wheels prevented them running off the far side. There was a small space fore and aft for the passengers and crew. We were pulled across by rope, one by one, and started off through the completely flat land, which was surrounded by high wire fences and their high, strong gates. Our host's *campinos*, twelve of them on horseback, met us. Each man wore a white shirt, long, white knitted stockings, leather shorts, green knitted cap and red jerkin. Each one carried on his saddle a leather apron as protection against bad weather and a scarf of bright colours, which is used to attract the bull's attention. They all had very long pikes which they held in their right hands, and their spurred feet were thrust into wooden stirrups shaped like small boats. Our host had changed into his riding clothes, a tall, broad-brimmed hat like a shortened top hat, a tight jacket with a fur collar, a leather apron over his trousers and gloves with gauntlets over his sleeves.

All seemed peaceful ; nothing was in sight but a few distant specks on the ranges. A gate was opened ; the *campinos* fanned out in front and on either side of us as our cars picked their way slowly over the grass. In front of us was an enclosure on the high wire fence. Against it a long platform was built up about three feet from the ground. The enclosure was made of iron sheets six feet high, and standing on the platform we looked down on a series of pens. All were fenced with iron, the first and last had gates opening on to the ranges, and each pen had a gate between it and the next. Outside the last one stood a small cart, like a miniature horse-box. The bull is driven into the box, which is just the size to hold him standing and so prevent his throwing himself about and hurting himself, and so is taken to his new destination.

FISH WOMEN AT NAZARÉ

FIELD WORKERS

CAMPINOS

OWNER OF BULLS

When we were all on the platform, the *campinos* opened
a gate and streamed through, riding towards a group of bulls
in the distance. Our host mounted his white bull-fighting
stallion. We had seen this wonderful creature on a former visit
to his house. It came out led by two men, and paraded up and
down before us with the airs and graces of a young and beautiful girl. Champion of many Portuguese bull-fights, it and its
rider seemed as one together ; they moved with grace and
smoothness and the most complete understanding. Our host's
son of eight was a small edition of his father, dressed in the same
way and mounted on a beautiful pony. He was not allowed
to join in the dangerous part of the display. As we watched,
the *campinos* fanned out, riding hard towards the distant bulls.
Our host leisurely went after them, his horse arching its neck
and stepping delicately, but with no outward excitement. The
bulls lifted their heads, saw the *campinos* and soon the range was
covered with charging bulls and fleeing men and horses. From
what looked like rout and disorder there quickly emerged a
picture : certain bulls were separated from their neighbours,
herded together and driven towards us, or, rather, they chased
the men towards us. As one man tired, another took his place,
shouting and waving his scarf to draw the furious bull in his
direction. Our host watched, completely detached, as if he and
his horse were watching something which did not concern them.
It seemed as if the men could not escape the furious rushes.
The long horns on the tossing heads were so near the horses'
flanks, yet each time the rider made a quick move and the bull
rushed on to charge empty space.

There was by now quite a crowd on our platform, men
and boys collected from nowhere, all shouting and applauding
any especially good show of riding. Still the white stallion and
its rider paced up and down in front of us as if it were in a show-
ring. There was a slight haze of dust over the mass rushing
towards us. Suddenly the white horse and its rider sprang
forward. The other riders parted, and our host faced the bulls
as they tore down upon him. He half turned and passed us,
flying ahead of the bulls. My heart nearly stopped when I saw
that he was charging towards a new herd which had suddenly
appeared in the distance. I gasped for a moment ; surely he
would be caught between the two, and what could he do against

those long murderous horns ? He had no pike with which to
fend off the bulls as his men had, but only his superb horsemanship and the complete understanding between him and his horse
with which to defend himself. The white stallion sped on till
it reached the new herd, which opened and the horse and its
rider passed through. The gap closed behind them and the herd
encircled the raging bulls. These were the bell cows. At once
the bulls quieted down ; still snorting and panting, they stopped.
The bell cows, gently guided by the men, who had gathered
like dogs on the outskirts of a fight, came towards us and the
whole of them poured into the first iron-ringed pen. At once
the doors clanged and the bulls, three or four of them, were
caught.

The excited audience, which grew larger each moment,
shouted, pointed and discussed the points of the huge creatures
just below them. The *campinos* dismounted and, using their
pikes, leaned dangerously over the high side and gradually
urged one beautiful fawn creature towards the door to the next
pen ; through it he charged, when it shut behind him, and he
stood just below us, his horns almost within touch of us, stamping
and snorting, his nostrils as red as fire. He stamped and snorted,
pawing the ground, then, whirling round like a flash of lightning,
charged the other side where some men and boys were shouting
at him. The whole place shook as his horns hit the iron, the men
on our side screamed at him, and he wheeled to charge again.
After a few moments the next gate opened and he flew through
it, to stamp and to snort unnoticed as the other bull—*the* bull
—was tempted towards the gate of the pen below us. He rushed
through it, and his speed brought him hard up against the far
side, where he stood banging and charging with short rushes. It
did not seem to hurt him and only the shouting crowd irritated
him. Once or twice a too-excited man threw his knitted cap
into the arena, to be stamped on instantly and torn to pieces.
This bull was pale brown. His horns curved up and out with
wicked points. His coat shone like satin ; the muscles moved
under the skin like ripples in water. He was the fiercest and the
best bull the ranch had produced for years, and his fate would
be the bull-ring in Madrid. At least he would give a good fight
before his life finished in glory. I hated to think that so much
beauty, strength and courage should be the sport of hundreds.

He was very precious and was not to be allowed to hurt or to tire himself.

The *campinos* mounted their horses again. Our host was in the centre of a wide circle facing the last gate. The door was opened and there stood the great bull for a moment, holding his head high and looking. Someone shouted, and like a streak of lightning, out he charged, making straight for the white stallion. Almost too quick for me to see, the horse turned and the bull tore after it, his horns so near the stallion's flank it seemed impossible for those sharp points not to catch it. The other bulls charged after him in every direction. Soon the range was covered with flying men, but nothing was done without purpose. Almost at once the design showed—to get the bulls back into their various ranges. The men fled shouting, waving their scarves and caps, making dashes at a bull if he seemed to turn towards another prey. Soon they were all specks in the distance on the great plain. The central white figure still rode, winding and twisting, turning, always just a few inches from the murderous horns, but at a given moment, with a wide swerve, he turned, the *campinos* closed in and the bull was surrounded by new quarries and quickly swept through a gate, which closed behind him, leaving him alone. A few rushes, which we could see, a stamp or two and he trotted off to his grazing. Peace settled down ; the men collected together, riding slowly back behind their master. The watching crowd melted, a few small boys stayed to see us get into the waiting cars, and we were off, bumping over the fields to the long white road which led us back to the river and home.

VIII

" QUINTAS " AND GARDENS

THE country houses—the *quintas*—of Portugal are one of the most distinctive and beautiful legacies of a great past, and Portugal is in many ways an ideal country for gardens. It is watered by great rivers in wide valleys, while tablelands and mountains shelter the country at their base from the east and leave it open to the fresh Atlantic breezes.

This small but varied land gives scope for many types of garden. When Philip II of Spain took possession of it in 1581, he wrote almost with envy to his daughters : " There are little gardens here in different parts which are not bad, and are called *alegretes*. We will get plans of them." The gardens of Penhalonga at Cintra pleased him too, and he writes : " They are pretty and there are numbers of them. There are lovely fountains which I would like to bring away with me."

I only know a few of the many gardens and *quintas* in Portugal. Those I saw gave me some idea of the beauty and grandeur of their past. With peace and age settled over them they still have a sense of spaciousness and order, and of their share in the life of the country. Many are cared for and lived in. Some, like Queluz, are, or were when I saw them, in the process of restoration, and their former glory is returning, while others are waiting, their loveliness half hidden in decay.

The great *Palacio* and *Quinta* of Bacalhoa lies in the shadow of the Serra d'Arrabida. The main road to Setubal and the south passes by it. The tiny village of Villa Fresca de Azeitão, with its fine Church of São Simão built in 1570 by the younger Albuquerque, is just outside the walls. Fountains near by are fed by the water from its tanks. Since the days of its greatness it has dominated the countryside with a quiet, loving grace— with the dignity of a great lady secure in her beauty—content to wait until understanding and knowledge should restore the splendour that was hidden for the time being.

Rasteiro, in his *Palacio e Quinta de Bacalhoa*, printed in Lisbon in 1895, says that it was built by the order of Dona Brites, mother

MATEUS, NEAR VILA REAL

MOORISH PAVILION AT BACALHOA

of Dom Manuel, in the last quarter of the fifteenth century. There is a mysterious palace built for João II, Dona Brites' son-in-law, by Andrea da Sansovino, which is spoken of by Vasari, but of which all traces have disappeared, and some believe that Bacalhoa may be the lost palace. This would account for some of the very early tiles or *azulejos* in the garden. Dona Brites did not keep it very long, as she gave it as a wedding present to her grandson, Dom Diogo, son of the Duke of Viseu, and in 1528 it was bought by Affonso Albuquerque the younger, natural son and heir of the great Admiral and Viceroy. It was after he had bought Bacalhoa that it was very likely altered to its present almost classical shape. Albuquerque had been to Italy in 1521 as a young man, in the train of another Dona Brites, when she came to Savoy as the Duke's bride. He is known to have travelled there, and must have learned to admire and later to imitate in some degree what he saw. On his return he bought Bacalhoa from the Infanta.

The house has corner turrets with melon - shaped roofs ; these and the balustrade on the entrance front are the only traces of baroque in its otherwise severe and classical appearance. The windows are square and there are three loggias, all with plain marble columns. The house is in one corner of the property and against it lies a formal box garden. This is of intricate design, and surrounds a fountain basin. Unlike most other Portuguese box gardens, there are no beds filled with flowers, but like the Italian gardens, it relies on the intricate pattern of the box planting for effect. It is one of the *giardini segreti* or *alegretes* mentioned by Philip II. The house surrounds the garden on two sides, with a high boundary wall on the third. A broad path under the wall leads to the great tank and Moorish pavilion at the end. Along this path are seats and tubs for orange trees. On these are the greatest variety of tiles and some of the earliest in the *quinta* ; they vary from Moorish in influence to classical. The walls are crowned with globes flanked by obelisks, and under these are medallions, very likely in imitation of the genuine Della Robbias on the wall above the tank. These imitations are fine examples of what local craftsmen can do if given works of art to copy. The wreaths round these medallions are inferior, but the heads are good. They represent historical figures from Alexander the Great to Nero. One is signed

5

" Donus Wilhelmus " (Master William), of whom nothing else is known.

From the house, as one stands in the loggia which faces west, the eye is carried over the busy box garden with its twists and curves, and the long, straight paths and orange trees, to the quiet water at the end. The pavilion facing the tank is hardly noticed until one is upon it, so close is it against the boundary wall. The three pointed roofs merge into one from the side, and not until one has turned and followed the edge of the great square water-tank does one see the grace of the front, the pointed roofs and rounded arches supported on severely plain columns of grey marble. Albuquerque very likely built this lovely pavilion. Inside all is cool and dark. The light from the water sends dancing shadows and patterns on the tile-covered walls and on the ceiling. The tiles here are very beautiful : some with conventional but naturalistic designs, others with pictures—Susanna and the Elders, and a fragment of the quarrel of Lapithæ and Centaurs. There is a small temple in the background of one tile, with the date 1565. These tiles may have been made in Spain as their design is very Spanish.

The tank is framed with tiles, and water flows into the centre from a dolphin. There are three empty niches in the wall above it, and between are four medallions of Della Robbia ware— two of men, two of women—most beautifully modelled and surrounded by glazed wreaths of fruit. These must have come from the Florentine factory, as they are of such beautiful workmanship and are like those seen in Northern Italy.

Bacalhoa passed through many hands, and when bought by its present owner in 1937 was in a state of neglect and decay, although it was a national monument. The outer walls stood thick and strong, a proof of the loving care that went to their building. The rounded towers at the corners with their baroque roofs showed strength, and above the severely plain portico, another legacy of Albuquerque, the heads of kings in niches looked down on the desolation below them. The pink marble columns of the loggia above the box garden were gone, but standing below in the tangle that was then the garden, one could see on the walls above the beautiful coloured tile pictures of the river gods, with their strapwork frames of blue and yellow.

Some of the floors in the rooms and most of their beautiful

wood ceilings were lying in decay as they had fallen into the cellars and to the ground floor. It looked an almost impossible task to restore it, but now it lives again, severe and beautiful in its cold simplicity. The pink marble columns from the western loggia were discovered under debris in a lower room. They were complete and unbroken, and now they stand to frame the view of the garden, the Moorish pavilion and water-tank at the end of it all.

The work of reconstruction has been done not only with loving attention, but with great knowledge. Local labour, working under the owner's eye and guidance, has brought it back to its perfection. The ceilings were replaced in the same style as before. When there was no guide in the room itself, ceilings from contemporary buildings were copied and the wood chosen with care. There are few or no plaster ceilings in old Portuguese houses. They are of panelled wood and are like *azulejos*, a legacy from the Moors adapted through the centuries to local needs, both in Spain and Portugal, though their design is seldom Moorish. Some are intricate, others rely for effect on the light and shade cast by the arrangements of plain surface and upholding beams. The entrance courtyard is still severe. More columns have been found, however, and are to be replaced as a colonnade facing the house where they had been in former times. The north side of the house has two loggias with grey marble columns cut in its face, one above the other. From these the view is over a wide country of wood, orange trees, olive and cork oaks, till it reaches the Tagus, beyond which lies Lisbon. On clear days the reflection of the sun on its many windows shines and winks at us across the distance, to where we watch from Bacalhoa.

Near Bacalhoa, between Sesimbra and Azeitão, is another *quinta*, the Quinta da Conceicão. It is decaying slowly and is neither as lovely nor as historical as its neighbours—but it is waiting for someone with vision and understanding to restore it to what it was. The land round it is farmed, and the big house is used by the peasants. The whole place is overrun with chickens and small children. Through the muddy courtyard you come to the entrance of the house, where you enter on the top floor, and on the far side the land falls away so that there are many large rooms on a lower level.

The house is long and low, E-shaped. The double row of steps to the front door is the centre bar of the " E." The steps curve widely to the huge doors, over which a small figure of the Madonna broods, waiting. On either side of the steps on the walls are large, life-size tile pictures of the guardians of its loneliness—two huge dogs drawn in vivid line and full of action. One dog is straining to reach and destroy the intruder, the other is smiling and friendly, for you have been to the house and are, therefore, welcome. It has many possibilities, and I longed to restore it to some of its former beauty.[1]

Calhariz, not far from Azeitão, is a baroque house in a restrained style. The country seat of the Duke of Palmella, in whose family it has been for over four hundred years, it lies south of the Tagus between Azeitão and Sesimbra and almost in the shadow of the Arrabida Mountains. Another white, E-shaped house, the fine baroque entrance doorway again makes the centre bar of the " E." The massive pillars on each side of it support a broken pediment, in the centre of which is a stone coat of arms surmounted by a crown. The stone used here is a deep mellow cream, in sharp contrast to the white of the house walls. The house itself is full of beautiful contemporary tiles. Those in the room of Battles are dated 1643, when the house was rebuilt. It has the usual formal box garden. Like so many large Portuguese country houses, it fits into the surrounding countryside as if it had grown there.

Queluz, which lies half-way between Lisbon and Cintra, has been a royal palace for some centuries. João IV, by the Charter of 17th August 1654, bestowed the property and its appurtenances on his son, the Infante Dom Pedro.

The lovely building which we now know was rebuilt between 1747 and 1786 by Joseph I for his son, Dom Pedro II ; contemporaries said in the manner of Versailles in miniature, but I could see no resemblance. The king employed native architects, who worked under the direction of the Frenchman, Jean Baptiste Robillion. The bill setting out the various items, for which Robillion charged him 829 milreis, is endorsed " Conta do Arquitecto. J. B. R." The baroque influence at Queluz is strong though restrained, and the whole is one of the most delightful efforts I know.

[1] I hear this *quinta* has now been bought and restored.

On the side where it is open to the road, the façade is simple in design, and relies for effect on the setting and proportion of the many green-shuttered windows, with their stone architraves and ornamentation. The whole is painted a faint pink. On the garden side it is more ornate. Here there is a centre block, above which is a balustrade and six statues. There are no shutters to the windows, but beautiful ironwork balconies lighten the façade where the stonework is more elaborate, though full of grace.

The interior, when I saw it, was in the process of restoration and all the lovely rooms were in workmen's hands. The most interesting was the one in which Pedro IV was born in 1798. It has medallions on the walls illustrating the life of Don Quixote. Other rooms have lovely yellow tiles with designs of fruit and trees. Another is papered with vivid pictures, but, though I went many times, I could never see these rooms properly. They were always partly covered by scaffolding and had men at work in them.

The overgrown gardens are terraced and are full of statues and fountains, as well as walls covered with fine *azulejos*. The river which feeds the fountains and canals is turned into a long tile-covered swimming-pool. These tiles picture a fleet of great ships in full sail. The pool was dry when I saw it, but I can imagine the cool delight of those ships seen through the clear water.

The proportions of these gardens are particularly good. To my mind they are far the finest piece of composite architecture that I saw in Portugal, and, in their way, one of the most enchanting garden designs in the world. Though in miniature, compared with other royal palace gardens they give an impression of spaciousness : conventional in design, yet they are full of surprises, delightful vistas and arrangements of trees, fountains, statues and steps. The palace and gardens are all part of the same scheme. They belong to each other, and together they produce the most satisfactory whole, one to which I returned again and again, with ever-growing pleasure. As I wandered, I thought of the visit Beckford paid there on a hot June night in 1787. His description of Queluz as it was then added to the mystery and enchantment of the place. He writes :

" The evening was now drawing towards its final close,

and the groves, pavilions and aviaries sinking apace into shadow : a few wandering lights sparkled amongst the more distant thickets—fire-flies perhaps—perhaps meteors ; but they did not disturb the reveries in which I was wholly absorbed.

" This night I began to perceive, from a bustle of preparation already visible in the distance, that a mysterious kind of fête was going forward ; and whatever may have been the leading cause, the effect promised at least to be highly pleasing. Cascades and fountains were in full play ; a thousand sportive *jets d'eau* were sprinkling the rich masses of bay and citron, and drawing forth all their odours, as well-taught water is certain to do upon all occasions. Amongst the thickets, some of which received a tender light from tapers placed low on the ground under frosted glasses, the Infanta's nymph-like attendants, all thinly clad after the example of her royal and nimble self, were glancing to and fro, visible one instant, invisible the next, laughing and talking all the while with very musical silver-toned voices."

Since I saw it last in 1939 I am told that the restoration is now complete, and the lovely place is back to its original ordered beauty—yet empty and without the faerie beauties which tantalized Beckford on that summer night.

To me, however, there was something fascinating in the semi-decay and wilderness of the neglected gardens, where one could wander and admire at will, with no tourist nor guide to disturb one's pleasure.

At Manique, on the Cintra side of Lisbon, loving hands have been at work. It was originally a Hieronymite convent, and all that remains of a very ancient past is the vast kitchen with hooded chimney and great stone table. At one end of the room is an old water sink of stone, and the walls are covered with very early tiles of Moorish design. The original small, round windows still exist, cut in the thick walls. All this has been carefully preserved. When the monks were expelled, the house was bought about one hundred years ago by the Marques das Minas, and it is still marked on maps as the Quinta do Marques das Minas. The rest of the house has been modernized, but is full of its original tiles. There are deep dados, all of different design, in each room. The earliest date from the seventeenth century, with broad bands of conventional design of Moorish influence, while in others the eighteenth-century tile pictures cover the lower part of the walls. In the dining-room, with its eighteenth-century tiles, are tall corner cupboards of fine proportion, which go from floor to ceiling, faintly baroque in influence. This influence is found again in the garden, where the walls are painted a deep pink and have mouldings, niches and busts in white, and water plays from baroque fountains and basins. Here everything is colour, in contrast to the sober greys and whites of Bacalhoa, and seems to glow with a hidden light of its own. The effect of this against the dark trees is startling. There are no views of open country here, but vistas through arches which lead from fountains to enclosed gardens and on to other fountains. The original convent was built next to the church, in which lies a body supposed to be that of St. Agatha, the patron saint of Catania and of nursing mothers. The body is preserved and can be seen at certain times. Agatha has her festival on 5th February. She was born in Sicily, probably in Catania, though Palermo also claims her, and was of noble birth and of great beauty. When she repelled the advances of the Roman prefect sent to govern Sicily by the Emperor Decius, she was brutally tortured at his orders, and sent to be burnt at the stake. As soon as the fire was lighted there was a great earthquake, and the people rose in an uproar to demand her release, but she died in prison on 5th February A.D. 251. Legend has it that Catania was saved by her veil from a great fire caused by the eruption of Mount Etna. How her body, if it is her body, came to Manique, I do not know and I could not find out.

Beyond Manique is Albarraque, which is not so old as Calhariz, but it is built on the site of a Moorish house. All that remains of the Moors is the deep well and water system with which the garden is irrigated. The house is white and solid, with no baroque influence. It is set in vines, and on the terrace are cut box bushes, a box garden and an arbour of pleached trees which shade a large stone table. The ground falls away below this to a wide view over stretches of wild country almost to the outskirts of Lisbon. In spring the countryside there is a sheet of colour. *Narcissi bulbocodium* grow thick as daisies on the grass, their tiny yellow petticoats bobbing in the wind. The stream at the bottom of the garden is bordered by heavy stones, and all through them the huge heads of *Scilla peruviana* thrust upwards—every shade from dark to pale blue.

The servants there were deeply interested in my plant-collecting, and often brought me some flower to see if it pleased me. At night they came to tell us they were going to their home in the garden cottage. Each one bowed before my host, his wife and then myself, with the wish, *Muita boa noite se Deus quizer* (" Good-night if God wills ").

The baroque influence shown in the garden walls and fountains at Manique is very strong in the *quinta* of the Conde de Vila Real at Mateus, near Vila Real. This is one of the finest examples of Portuguese baroque in the whole country. The low white house is built round three sides of a square, and encloses a narrow forecourt. The entrance to the court is through an ornate balustrade. The centre of the building is elaborately carved and completely baroque in character, while the wings are more severe in style, with classical windows and doorways. There is an extraordinary number of tall finials which rise from the roof, a feature peculiar to Portuguese architecture. The house is painted white, while the stone used for the carving of window-frames, balustrades, doorways and pilasters at the corners is a deep cream-yellow. The façade of the church which adjoins the house is also baroque in character, in strong contrast to the quiet simplicity of the interior. There is a garden of box-bordered flower-beds on one side of the house, and here the whole façade is severe and simple, with the exception of the finials on the corners of the roof and church tower. I found these box gardens at nearly all the *quintas* I saw.

From Bacalhoa we drove south to the rich country of the Alemtejo, passing on our way the rice lands beyond Alcacer-do-Sol, and so on to Estremoz.

In Estremoz I found that life at the Quinta do Carmo was completely patriarchal. Almost everything that we ate, drank and used, grew or was made on the property. I think I am right in saying that sugar, salt, tea and coffee were practically the only things that had to be bought for the house. The blankets were made of home-grown wool, the linen of home-grown flax—everything came from the property. The great white house a few miles out of Estremoz faced its many out-buildings across a wide lawn. This lawn ended in a wall pierced by an iron gate covered with wistaria. Beyond was a garden filled with native and English plants, with a pavilion at the end. In the house the tall white rooms were cool and shuttered against the sun. The walls were covered with eighteenth-century *azulejos*. The chapel at the end of it was reached by a private door as well as a large one which opened on to the lawn.

Facing the house, the great out-buildings were full of the various stores from the property. In one were huge vats for the grapes, hogsheads of wine, oil, vinegar, and in an open tank was the residue of the grapes after wine-making, a purple mass which is used for dyeing. Each vineyard on the property produced a different wine. One was particularly delicious and was called burgundy for lack of a better name. We liked it so much we persuaded our host to let us take some back to England. The transport of it was difficult, for it was in huge hogsheads which were usually disposed of locally or to France, as Portuguese wine was sold there in large quantities to be used for blending. It was impossible for me to take the hogsheads back with me, but when I did return home I had a garish peasant's trunk made of wood covered with painted tin, and closely packed with bottles of wine from Estremoz. There are many very good wines made in Portugal besides port, and it seems a pity that they are not better known. Amongst them are *Colares* and *Busaco*, red and white. Occasionally one can find a delicious sparkling Busaco, but it is rare. There is also an excellent Portuguese brandy.

It was Easter time at Estremoz, and in the yard behind the wine lodges we saw a small flock of black lambs. Each family on the great property had its Easter lamb or part of one, and the priest who served Mass in the chapel shared with them. Coming back through the yard later in the day, the poor little things had met their fate, and we saw them as they lay in rows waiting to be given away. In Estremoz itself the market was in progress, and wherever we went our host was surrounded by peasant and farming friends, all with some boon to ask and all to go away seemingly satisfied. His pockets were filled with the Easter sugared almonds, and all the children had a handful as they pressed round him.

Of all the market stalls and shops the saddler's was the most fascinating. It was full of bright colour ; ropes for traces and halters were made in red and yellow and hung in long bunches from the ceiling. I found them charming and useful to use as hand-rails on a staircase. The wide white harness webbing was covered with a conventional design in red, blue and yellow. My son had a buckle added to a short piece and it made a delightful belt. The harness was studded with brass nails and was full of colour from tufts of bright wool ; and the whole shop was as gay as a Christmas tree.

In the side streets were the potters, at work on primitive wheels turned by their feet. They were making large and small pots, some of a black ware with a high glaze, others for water-jars, so porous that water standing in them is quickly cooled by the evaporation through their skins.

At Estremoz as well as Elvas the delicious Elvas plums are made, mostly in small factories. Many *quintas* make some of them for their own consumption. They were very cheap and we bought several large boxes for the price of a small one in England.

From high up on the walls of Elvas you look towards Spain, with Badajoz in the distance, and below flows the river Guadiana, which is the boundary between the two countries. Wellington's fortifications still stand there, strong and wide. Over the gate facing Spain, in his niche, the tiny figure of a British Grenadier keeps guard. So little of England remains in Portugal after the long years of fighting and building in the Peninsular Wars. The lines of Torres Vedras can still be seen, and the additions to the fortifications at Elvas, but little else. I said this to a friend in Lisbon while watching a party of soldiers on some festival and his answer was :

" Did you hear the order to the cavalry when they rode off? It was *Terrot*," and he told me that " Trot " was not the only command still given in English. The orders to the sentries on changing guard and all the bugle-calls are still those of the British Army of Peninsular War days.

At Quinta do Carmo all the products of the various Reynolds' properties are collected and distributed. I only saw one of their outlying *quintas*. The road led us through cork woods till we came to where it stopped. Then a team of mules met us and we were pulled through the mud and ruts until we came to firm ground again. Here were fields where the breeding mares lived with their foals, and the game farm where pheasants were bred to be sent all over the country. The farmer and his family crowded round the car. Lunch was waiting for us in a large, airy room hung with guns. Everywhere there were children watching to see if our host had remembered the Easter almonds. There was no pushing or begging. Each child came forward with its hand cupped to receive the gift and to run away afterwards, happy with its prize. Sugared almonds are the traditional gift to all friends and dependants at Easter time.

Wherever we went through the flat lands of the Alemtejo were the great cork woods, miles of forest broken by stretches of cultivated fields. The women working in tree fields and woods have an amusing way of tying their skirts round their legs, and they look as if they were wearing rather short peg-topped trousers which are tucked into their boots. With their large hats to shade them from the sun they seem top heavy, but the whole effect is very workmanlike and practical.

There is a great difference between a well and a badly managed cork forest. The care with which the bark is cut varies, and in consequence the trees are shapely and well furnished or starved and twisted. The newly barked trees stand brown and smooth, their stems like velvet, next to the corrugated greyness of those still to be done. There is, or should be, a strict rotation in the barking : so much time between each, so that the tree is not weakened. The bark is taken to the cork factories, where it is pressed and treated in the way that was invented a century ago by the original Reynolds to settle in Portugal. He found that corks for the port bottles were made from any thick bark that could be found, and that it was difficult to get sufficient for the growing wine trade. His invention for the treating of cork is still in use to-day at the Reynolds factory.

Between Evora and Estremoz is the high ground of the Serra d'Ossa, covered with olives, cork trees and vines. Passing through Redondo to a small village, Aldeia da Serra, we turned up a rough cart-track and plunged into the cork woods. The track was bad and steep and got worse as we crawled up it, the car turning from side to side as its wheels fell into deep ruts, first to left and then to right. There was no view, only the close, narrow valley as we climbed, but we knew that hidden away on the hillside was the beautiful Convento da Serra d'Ossa.

This late sixteenth-century house is built on the site of a much earlier one, and was added to in the middle of the eighteenth century. Once filled with teeming life, it is now empty, its courtyards falling into decay, the huge lower refectories crowded with casks and bins which hold the harvest from the property. The rest is empty rooms and echoing passages. Behind the building are many courtyards with fine fountains against *azulejos*-covered walls. The most beautiful is in the main passage—a fluted shell on a base of acanthus leaves, while dolphins spout water into the basin. It is baroque and secular in design, as are most of the fountains in this convent. In the eighteenth century another house was built where the farmer now lives. Below it are terraces and on the lowest of these is the great water-tank, without which no *quinta* garden seems complete. In the summer heat it is cool under the orange trees that overhang, and are reflected back by, the water. In this way the Portuguese gardens resemble those I saw in Persia, where there was always a pool or stream.

Wandering through the deserted convent rooms, we came to an open window. Below on the entrance terrace trees had surrounded us, so we had no warning of the beauty that lay below until we looked out over the woods and the low hill in front to the vale of Evora. The sky was threatening. Dark clouds cast their shadows on the country, which stretched for miles into the distance where the low hills melted in a blue-grey haze that might be the sea. As the clouds moved, the colours changed from grey to green. The sun shone through at moments, sending down shafts of golden light which were quickly extinguished as the clouds sped on, only to break through again and to change everything they touched for a few minutes to green and dazzling beauty. The impression left on me was of great sadness, when we finally turned away down the narrow road. So much beauty, so much life and history, hidden in the great walls, and now, neglect and ruin everywhere. The house was alive still, but the sleep of death and decay was not far off.

If Bacalhoa is severely classical in shape, while Queluz and Mateus are baroque, Bemfica is by contrast completely individualistic, and owes, in the house itself, little to what went before or came after it was built. This was in the seventeenth century, when the Marquez de Fronteira, the friend of the poet, Luis de Sousa, wanted a country house and chose the beautiful valley of Alcantara for its site. The house was altered and added to in the eighteenth century, with more regard to comfort than to correct architectural style. It is now full of many treasures, the collections of nearly three centuries, but it is the garden which makes Bemfica unique. The great house faces a large formal box garden divided into squares by two broad paths which cross in the centre. At their intersection is the largest of five fountains. Thus divided, it is again broken into a series of smaller parterres, each with geometrical box-bordered flower-beds, which surround a central fountain or basin.

There are many classical statues on pedestals along the wider paths, and some fine cut box trees and palms which shade seats at the far end, from where one can look back across flower-filled beds to the rose-pink house with its white doors, columns and surrounds to the windows.

The most interesting and unusual feature of this entrancing place is the long water-tank, which is the boundary of the garden on one side, as the sheltering walls and the house are the boundaries of the other three. The water is separated from the garden by a high stone balustrade of fine design. In it stand two baroque statues. The far wall of the tank is tall and has three openings, between which are panels of *azulejos*, pictures of men on horseback. Above this again is a narrow terrace with the same balustrade as below, and the wall here is broken by niches painted a dark red, and in them, in sharp contrast, are white busts of kings and emperors. This terrace is reached by wide flights of steps at each end of the tank. They rise to meet the façades of two summer-houses with pointed hipped roofs. Near the house is another wall with more tiles and statues at intervals.

Though certain features may remind one of gardens in Italy and Spain, yet the entire effect at Bemfica is absolutely Portuguese, for nowhere else could one see such a delightful combination of the great national speciality—the *azulejos* or tile picture—combined with the sober grey stone of basin, steps and balustrade, and the colour of the garden flowers blended into a whole by the deep green of the box-border hedges.

I feel that here I must tell a little of the history of the *azulejos*, which I mention so often in describing these Portuguese

houses and gardens.   The word and the tiles which are so called
are of Moorish origin.   *Azulejos* may be derived from the Arabic
azzullaja or *azulaish*, meaning " smooth."

The earliest tiles were those left by the Moors.   Their
technique of outlining the patterns by raised edges went out of
fashion in the fifteenth century.   From then the design was out-
lined in dark blue painted flat on to the tile.   Early in the
sixteenth century there came into use pictures painted in naturalistic colours on many tiles, which were then joined into a whole
—notably the work done by Francisco de Mattos.   Moorish
geometrical patterns were used almost exclusively till the end of
the fifteenth century, but the Renaissance changed these severe
designs and the tiles were now made in great variety, many
classical, others realistic, such as some at Bacalhoa, where there
are octagons with classical borders surrounding green and blue
leaves.

The colours changed with the designs.   After the earliest and
rare Moorish patterns in black there followed those in blue,
green and brown with a little yellow.   When the tiles became
westernized, though the technique was still Moorish the colours
remained the same except for brown, which is seldom seen.
Later green and brown disappeared, leaving blue and yellow,
until in the eighteenth century the tiles which had now become
parts of large pictures were always in blue and white.   These
pictures are often surrounded by a highly ornate border or
frame of baroque influence.   I have seen many of these pictures,
which show perfectly the contemporary life at the date they were
made—houses, furniture, dress, gardens, boar and other hunts.

In the sacristy of the church of Madre de Deus there is a vivid
picture of an avenue of trees disappearing into a faint distance.
The old caretaker's pleasure is to stand you in different parts of
the church and, from wherever you look, it seems that the vista
is facing you and asking you to step down it.

In the kitchen of a *quinta* not far from Lisbon the plaster
walls are broken by realistic pictures of game, birds, hares, a
huge ham, a side of pork and ribs of beef, all in tiles.   In exactly
life size these are set in the plaster as if hanging there until wanted.
In these later tiles there is a strong Dutch influence.

These pictures are still made, but the blue is not as good
and the designs are more conventional and commercialized

instead of being, as in the early ones, the work of some native artist.

A very typical feature of both the gardens and roadsides as well as the city streets is the fountains. In a country where there is such a long, dry summer, the question of water is of the greatest consequence. This has been made available from early times by the many fountains, so arranged that the overflow of the drinking water is for animals. There are sometimes large basins to be used for washing linen. The vision of the donors, for most of them were given by local landowners, have made them things of beauty quite apart from their utility. Many of them have certain features in common. They are nearly all monumental, with very varied outlines, and are set against a house or wall. The arms of their donors often form part of the design, which is baroque, and the drinking water flows from the mouths of grotesque masks. Some of these are crowned, such as those outside Bacalhoa, others have high foreheads, but all have big ears. In the country the wall against which the fountain is placed is part of the design, and here the variations are great. Near Azeitão is the only one I know which is completely in polycrome. This has pictures of eighteenth-century gallants on either side of an extremely plain basin, and the more ornate pediment has the bust of a woman painted in lifelike colours, while at Bacalhoa is a very simple variety of the usual design coloured a faint rose-pink, with only the basin, pillars and top moulding of deep cream stone. A Judas tree in full bloom hung over the wall at its side one day in April, the cream, pink and pale purple mingled against a sky of the deepest blue. Near Elvas there is the fountain of Nossa Senhora da Piedade, to which comes a pilgrimage yearly on 21st to 22nd September. This is quite different from others, for its long trough has only two masks, one at each end, and is at the base of three *azulejos* pictures.

The two fountains that attracted me the most were at Arraiolos and Montemor o Nove, both in the Alemtejo. At Arraiolos the ornate white semicircular wall is broken by arches on either side of the big oval water-basin. Above each arch are tall points crowned by moulding and rounded finials, and above the drinking fountain the wall rises again into a fan-shaped design of raised carving, above which is the coat of arms of either

the donor or of the village. The whole is set against the hillside
with a fringe of cork trees.

The fountain at Montemor has the same white walls, but
the centre is broken by coloured plaques with some of the
mouldings picked out in colour, and there are seats at the base
where the weary traveller can rest after a refreshing drink.
Many of these fountains are on long stretches of lonely road
miles from a village and are a great help to the travellers—man
and beast.

Going from *quinta* to *quinta* near Lisbon and in some places
south of the Tagus, we saw many hills crowned by little, round,
white windmills with pointed tiled roofs and strange, short
sails, very wide at the top and tapering to nothing at the base.
Sometimes there were rows of them all close together like tiny
forts which had found a new usefulness. They grind the corn
between their ancient stones in the same primitive fashion that
has been in use for centuries.

At one the miller and his son worked by themselves. With
his knitted cap well pulled down over his ears, each watched and
guided the corn into the hopper that fed the stones, and again
the coarse flour that resulted into the sacks. The miller was
just having his midday meal when we put our heads in at the
door. He greeted us with charming politeness. " Yes, he would
gladly show us everything." I climbed the tall ladder and
watched the corn fall, be caught in the grinder and come out
again to fall into the waiting sacks. The miller was full of
curiosity. " Had the senhora never seen a mill before ? His
was only one of many. Alas ! times were bad, as the new-
fangled power-driven mills ground finer flour, though not
nearly as good and as healthy as that from the old stone mills.
Still, people were foolish and in the cities liked white bread,
which did not feed them in the same way. Look what a good
meal he had. Bread from his own flour, vegetable soup and his
own wine. Would not the senhora have some of it ? " He
offered me his bowl of soup, thick with many vegetables—a
thin skin of oil floated on the surface—and a bottle of wine.
There was no plate nor any flask to drink from, so we regret-
fully refused, whereupon he solemnly drank our health, holding
the bottle high and pouring the wine down his throat without
swallowing it at all. The bottle never touched his lips.

It is a pity these mills are being superseded by the modern commercial mill, for it is quite true that the flour they grind, though coarse, is delicious with a nutlike flavour, and contains all the essential parts of the grain. Again, Portugal has always been the country of craftsmen. Their furniture is nearly always hand made, their carpets, either worked on canvas or woven, blankets, straw mats, pottery, all show the difference of workmanship and design, though this is nearly always an ancient one modified by each individual. To exchange this for modern mass-production is to lose an artistic heritage, and I hope it will be long before the small craftsman, working on his own, will be overwhelmed by the wave of modern " improvements."

IX

PLANTS AND PLANT-COLLECTING IN PORTUGAL

FOR anyone who likes the simple life, with charming courtesy and help from everyone, the weeks spent in out-of-the-way parts of Portugal plant-collecting will be a joy and a revelation. The first indication I had of what spring could be like there was early in March. The road followed the sea for miles beyond the last village. On one side the Atlantic stretched wide and smooth as silk to the horizon, the slow heaving rollers surged towards the rocky shore ; they rose and fell to break with a sudden roar, dragging stones and sand back to the sea as they receded. On the other side grew the pine forests, planted centuries ago by King Diniz to stop erosion of the coast and to shelter the country beyond from the Atlantic gales. Between was a broad strip of land where outcrops of stone broke the surface and made a natural rock garden, planted in bold and sweeping groups of colour which mingled at the edges. The deep blue of *Lithospermum* with the pink and white of Campions (*Silene*), and stretches of the naturalized *Mesembryanthemum* with soft yellow flowers. The mass of colour would suddenly be broken by patches of silver-grey Everlasting (*Helichrysum*), Thrift, though not in flower, made height with rounded tufts, Asphodels of all kinds sent up spikes of pink and white, mysterious bunches of leaves were the promise of an Autumn Crocus (*Colchicum lusitanicum*) and, in pure sand, grew the large bulbs with almost exotic leaves of the Sea Lily (*Pancratium maritimum*), whose fragrant white flowers do not show till June. On the edge of the wood and coming down to the road like a thick carpet were *Cistus* of all kinds, white, purple and pink, and great patches of gorse were in flower and filling the air with a hot, heavy scent. This was only a glimpse of what the flora of Portugal could do when spring had returned.

The plants one collects for English gardens must be acclimatized, for they dislike our climate at first. Even those from the Estrela Mountains, where snow lies on into April, hate our damp frosts, continual thaws and variation of temperature in winter. They miss the long, dry summer and the baking they get. I lost many through trusting them to the open ground without giving them a chance to adapt themselves to the vagaries of our climate, and I think they should be kept in a cold Alpine house or in a frame for at least a year after they are brought back. During the limited time that I had, and the small amount of ground which I covered, I found nothing new, but many lovely plants which were well worth this extra trouble.

I went first to the Serra d'Arrabida, which is a natural rock garden. There *Arbutus unedo* grew thickly, their tiny green-white flowers and red fruit both hanging near each other. Their smooth red stems shone like satin in contrast to the dark green of their leaves. There were great drifts of Rosemary and Lavender (*L. Stœchas*), which scented the air with a dry, spicy smell. *Cistus* of all sorts were on every sunny bank or slope, some with satin-white flowers which had at the base of each petal a dark red blotch, *C. ladaniferus*, others purplish red, *C. crispus*, a pale purple, *C. albidus*, various white forms of *C. salvifolius* and *C. monspeliensis*, with many hybrids between these two, so that the whole hillside was a sheet of white, pink and purple, with the green-grey-leaved and yellow-flowered *Helianthemum* in between the various groups. There must be many good hybrids to be found if one is blessed with the seeing eye of the true plant-collector.

Captain Collingwood Ingram collected elsewhere in Portugal a most beautiful new species of *Cistus* with huge white flowers and shining dark green leaves, which he has called *Palhinhaii*. He also found in Spain a variety of *C. ladaniferus* with flowers far larger and more perfect in shape than any I have seen.

On Arrabida, as well as much farther south, there were as many species of these shrubby *Helianthemums* as of *Cistus*, and again there must be many hybrids, some of which should have the good points of both parents. The most common was *H. formosum* and its varieties. It has a deep yellow flower with a brown blotch at the base of each petal, and the grey-green leaves make a thick mat of intertwining branches. *H. alyssoides* spread over the ground and rose to two or three feet covered with pure yellow flowers. There was *Helianthemum ocymoides*, taller than its neighbours and less free, with its flowers of deep yellow. Its leaves when young are covered with down and are almost white, but become green as they grow older. The young shoots with their tender leaves against the older, deeper coloured ones give the plant an effect of shot silk. There were various forms of *Helianthemum vulgare*—our Rock-Rose—creeping in lowly places. *Lithospermum apulum* covered the rocks with dark tight leaves and deep blue flowers, and through it grew *Gladiolus segetum* in lovely contrast, with spikes of bloom which varied from a dullish pink to a wine purple. On Arrabida and elsewhere the beautiful Blue Pimpernel (*Anagallis linifolia*) had flowers the size of small Gentians and of the same deep, vivid blue ; it was of a strong and shrubby growth and spread over many feet of ground. By

the roadside a mist of blue was *Iris Sisirynchium*. Its flowers die with the sun, and, passing by next day, the ground is blank, but the miracle of blue returns a day or two later, making an ever-changing carpet of colour.

I found *Tulipa australis* var. *lusitanica* on Arrabida as well as elsewhere south of the Tagus, growing in almost unbelievably hard ground. As I hacked away, trying to get a few bulbs, I thought of my efforts in Persia, where sometimes bulbs were buried two feet or more in soil that was almost rock, with only a thread-like stem to bring life to the plant above. The tulips were not so deeply buried on Arrabida, though it took great effort to secure them. *Narcissus bulbocodium* grew there, both on the high, dry hilltops and in the low valleys. Coutinho lists several forms of this enchanting Petticoat Daffodil. I found it in many places and its habit varied accordingly—small with short stem on the high, dry uplands, tall with large trumpets in the damp lowlands, and again in cultivated fields the height varied according to the soil.

The wild Stock (*Matthiola tristis*), in the driest spots on Arrabida, starved for water, was only a few inches high, but transplanted to a friend's garden it grew to two feet and was covered thickly with upright heads of pale mauve. *Pæonia mascula* grew amongst rocks in damp dells with Solomon's seal and *Helleborus fœtidus* as companions. The yellow-green of their leaves and flowers made a perfect setting for the glowing crimson of the Peony's large yellow-centred cup. Unfortunately I asked some children if they knew where it grew and, without waiting for me, they dashed away to return with armfuls of the torn and ravished plant. It nearly broke my heart to think of the harm done in their efforts to please. To make it worse, most of what they brought was useless either for herbarium specimens or to grow. It taught me a lesson, and from that time on I only asked to be shown a plant growing in its natural setting.

In Lisbon and all along the country roads in May are children carrying for sale great bunches of the yellow " Lirio amarello dos montes," *Iris lusitanica*. It is a pity this lovely thing should be so popular, as the extensive picking must in time lessen the range of its growth, if it is never allowed to seed. I was enchanted to see its deep yellow heads rising out of the growing corn or on the rocky heath-covered slopes. South of the Tagus I found several of its pale blue variety, but these were rare and not nearly as beautiful, though more delicate in colouring. Another flower growing wild and sold by the roadside was *Adonis autumnalis* var. *bæticus*, called locally " Lagrima de sangue " (tears of blood). The small red stars surrounded by the feathery leaves look just like drops of blood.

The deep purple of the somewhat squat rhizomitous *Iris biflora*, the " Lirio roxo," was over before *Iris lusitanica* had started. It grew thickly north of Lisbon and its great heads seemed top-heavy for their short stems and leaves. Near it were many orchis, some of which were almost the earliest flowers I saw. As I was not collecting them, I have none of their names, but they were all beautiful and their varieties were legion. There were many *Ornithogalums*, ranging from the Star of Bethlehem, which we all know (*Ornithogalum umbellatum*), to the tall

O. narbonense, and in the far north I found the tiny *O. unifolium* growing in less than an inch of soil on slabs of rock. One wondered how it could live and prosper with so little to feed and cover it. They are a satisfactory bulb, for the different varieties I saw covered a long flowering period. Again on Arrabida and nowhere else did I find the white candytuft (*Iberis sempervirens*) ; it grew only in one spot, and was lovely in conjunction with the deep blue of a near-by *Anagallis*. On the dry tops of the Serra, as well as in the valleys near Setubal, grew the lovely sage (*Phlomis purpurea*) in great masses. It looks like a pinky-mauve version of *Phlomis fruticosa.*

Some plants and bulbs are very local and the Tagus seems to be a dividing-line over which they do not cross to go either north or south. This was so with birds as well ; one instance is the Blue Magpie " Charneco " (*Cyanopica cyanus cooki*), which is found only here and in Central and Southern Spain. It is interesting to note that this species in its typical form is not seen again until we reach China and South-East Asia. The purple *Phlomis* did not grow in the north, nor did certain *Cistus Helianthemums, Tulipa australis* and the broom-like *Retama monosperma*, which I only found at Troia, though it grows in the Algarve. The greatest treasure of all, which also does not cross the great river, is the snowflake (*Leucojum trychophyllum*). I first saw a few of its shining white bells under some pines not far from Setubal. It seemed completely out of place, so perfect, so delicate and so fragile, growing in such rough and arid soil, for under the pines it was pure sand and rocks. Each graceful stem a few inches high had several tiny bells, some pure white, others with a faint tinge of pink at the base, others had a touch of green. A few days later I came upon thousands of them growing, this time in the sparse shade of the cork woods and in the same light, dry soil. When happy they invaded the edge of the road and even grew amongst the piles of gravel left by the roadmen. Near them was *Anemone palmata*, with butter-yellow flowers, some tinged with pink on the outside of the petals. Occasionally I found a few of these Anemones, which were a delicious creamy white. They deeply resented transplanting and I could get no seed.

Farther north the earliest bulbs I saw were *Narcissus tazetta* (paper white), thin carpets of the crocus-like Romulea, followed by Scillas of every size and shape. *Scilla peruviana* grew under walls and stones, its big bulbs buried two feet deep in the hard, dry ground.   The colours of its large, round heads varied from Cambridge blue to a deep purple. I believe it is sometimes found pure white, but I never saw this.   In the woods going north to Coimbra were masses of a tiny blue gem only three inches high—*Scilla verna*.   We found it again later in the spring high up in the northern mountains, where there was a slope thickly carpeted with it, and pushing through and amongst its blue bells were the slender stems and pale yellow trumpets of the angels' tears (*Narcissus triandrus*)—a most lovely natural planting. *Narcissus cyclamineus* grew in damp valleys and near streams. I only found the four Narcissi—*N.N. tazetta, bulbocodium, triandrus and cyclamineus*, though there are others in more out-of-the-way places.   The Alliums were out at the same time as *Iris lusitanica*. There was a very pretty small-headed pink one with its rare white variety. *Fritillaria lusitanica* grew amongst the heath. It was difficult to see its soft brown-spotted head until one was almost upon it, so well was it camouflaged and one with its surroundings.   It is very like its northern relation, *F. pyrenaica*, but has not the horrible musty smell which makes *pyrenaica* so disagreeable near by.   The only Grape Hyacinth that I saw had an ugly spiky flower, I think *Muscari neglectum*.

As spring advanced, the broom burst into yellow fire and with it the many species of gorse, small, prostrate and tall. I was too early to get any seed. Not only broom and gorse set the country aflame, but also wonderful *Echium* (*E. plantagineum*), a deep red with a blue tip. Sometimes the fields, where it grew amongst the crops, looked almost blood red, when a sudden breeze would turn the flowers to make a mist of reddy purple as the two colours merged in the distance. In other fields there were so many bright and colourful flowers growing there seemed little room for the crops. In one I listed all in flower, *Chrysanthemum coronarium, Ornithogalum narbonense, Arctotis calendulacea, Gladiolus segetum, Nigella*—both white and blue—*Calendula arvensis, Anchusa*, white convolvulus and a deep red annual poppy. The black blotch at the base of its petals makes a perfect crusader's cross, hence the local name, Crusader's Poppy. There was the bright blue of Chicory, several Vetches, *Asperula aristata*, a particularly deep almost red Mallow (*Malva hispanica*, I believe),

Grape Hyacinths, *Centauria vicentina*, *Cynoglossum* and the Scarlet Pimpernel (*Anagallis tenella*), growing nearly as strong and large as its blue sister. There was a huge pink-flowered Dock which I did not get named, and the lovely blue of *Linum narbonense*. This was only one day's flowering, but a short time later another set of flowers would take their place and keep the succession and colour going until the whole countryside was burned brown by the hot sun and strong Atlantic summer gales.

The heaths, too, were legion. The hills behind Lisbon and Estoril are covered with them, and they are frequent from the Minho to the Algarve. Here again there must be many good forms of *Erica* to be found among the species *E.E. arboria, mediterranea* and *lusitanica*. Some flowers are very local in their distribution. Cabo da Roca seemed to have several things which I did not find elsewhere, though they may grow in places which I did not visit. The most notable was the giant white thrift, *Armeria Welwitschii*, of which I was lucky enough to get some seeds, which have come true. Then there was the tiny *Dianthus gallicus* var. *lusitanica*, which would have been easy to pass by but for the delicious scent from its rather small ragged flowers—a scent that set one searching to find its host. A list of the plants seen one morning on this fascinating point were *Cistus albidus, C. salvifolius* and their hybrids, the *Dianthus*, *Helichrysum fœtidum*, a blue lupin with deeply cut almost fringed leaves, I believe *Lupinus angustifolius*, *Echium*, several species of *Campanula*, *Helianthemums*, both shrubby and creeping, *Calendula*, *Anthemis* in variety, *Chrysanthemums* and a huge-headed umbelliferæ like a yellow Hemlock, wine-red Snapdragon (*Anterrhinum*), Foxgloves, *Astragalus* and *Crambe Hispanica*, the beautiful white Thrift and *Lychnis coronaria*.

Packing the bulbs and plants which I had collected was a difficulty. I had come out unprepared for all the treasures I was to find, and had nothing in which to bring them back to England safely. Some had been growing in the Legation garden for some months after I had collected them ; others, such as bulbs, were not properly dried off, and I feared that on the several days' journey home by sea they would suffer. I needed some waterproof container in which to keep them happy in my cabin. My host one day, with a twinkle in his eye, gave me a large parcel marked " Lufthansa," which he told me had been given him by Count Beroldingen—head of the German Air Company, but really the principal Nazi in Portugal. Bertie had explained my difficulty, and the Count at once gave him a lot of the small bags which are given to air-sick passengers at the start of a rough flight, and most perfect they were for the plants and bulbs, who did not seem to mind their long journey when packed in such comfortable quarters !

I am afraid this is a sparse list of only some of the plants I saw in a three months' visit, during which I was able to cover a very small part of the rich ground. I only hope I may have given a slight picture of what can be seen there during the early and late spring. What I do hope most seriously is that the country will not be ravished of its great horticultural treasures. I have purposely not said where some of these can be found, nor will I tell anyone, for the commercial collecting of plants and bulbs, as well as that by thoughtless amateurs, has led in some other countries to the practical destruction of their native flora, and some governments have imposed legislation to try and save what is still left. No real plant-lover will ravish a colony, but will take the greatest care to pick and choose so that few gaps will be left after he has been, and he will see that the plants have every chance to increase, to the pleasure and satisfaction of those who come after. My botanical data was given me on the spot, and has been verified from Professor Antonio Coutinho's *Flora de Portugal*.

Plant-collectors should remember that in order to bring their collections into England a permit from the Board of Agriculture and Fisheries is necessary. This is a safeguard against disease.

X

THE STORY OF PORTUGAL

THE evolution of Portugal from a county of the Iberian Peninsula of Roman days into a separate nation, with customs, language and strong sense of nationality, is a fascinating one.

Of the early inhabitants little is known. They may well have been of Celtic origin from the few words that have survived, and the many rough stone monuments like those which were left by primitive peoples all over Europe. Between Braga and Guimarães is the city of Citania, which crowns the hill high above the road between these two places. In the museum at Guimarães there is a great stone which was taken from Citania. This links the inhabitants of that city to the early Celts, if the carvings and symbols on it have been rightly interpreted.

It is in the shape of a pentagon and each side measures about five feet. In the middle of one there is a semicircular hollow. The surface of the stone has many grooves converging to one point. The rest of it is carved with intricate patterns, which resemble those on Celtic stones in Scotland.

For many years it was believed to be a sacrificial altar, but a few years ago, during the excavations of a road to Citania, two other stones, of the same type but less ornate in decoration, were discovered in position as the fronts of small, very unusual buildings, the use of which is in doubt, for they are certainly not dwelling-houses.

At Citania there are curious round buildings and a few square, all built of granite blocks with only one entrance, a door, which is often surrounded by rough carvings. A few coins and inscriptions show that the city was in existence from the early Bronze Age, through most of the Roman occupation. Though it was inhabited when St. James is supposed to have preached at Braga, then Bracara Agusta, there are few traces of Christianity amongst the ruins. Some early lidless granite coffins, which surround a cross of later date, are all that suggest a few inhabitants who had followed in the steps of their Roman neighbours and adopted the new religion, but this, too, is only supposition. During those early days there was also a continual *va et vient* of the Phœnicians, who have left such strong traces of their passage all along the coast.

The Romans did not occupy the whole of what is now Portugal—their land of milk and honey—until the reign of Augustus, two hundred years after they had begun to colonize the country. They stayed for over four hundred years, leaving the language as their chief monument. There are also the beautiful remains of a temple at Evora, which in the Middle Ages, was used as a slaughter-house, but which has now been restored, and milestones, pavements and tombstones at various places.

Christianity had come to Portugal before the Romans left in the fifth century, and already religious intolerance had caused much suffering. The Vandals and Goths, who swept over the country in 417, were not converted to Christianity for many years, and the orthodox, who had persecuted their erring brothers, were themselves persecuted. The Vandals passed on to Africa, leaving the whole land to the Goths and Suivis, who first occupied all the country north of the Tagus as well as part of Spain. They have left practically no traces of their occupation except in an occasional broad-faced Germanic type amongst the peasantry.

As rulers they were very unpopular, and the country people did little or nothing to resist the great wave of Moslem invasion which swept over the land in 711. Defeating King Roderick at Guadalete, the Moors, as they were called, reached the northern mountains very quickly. Here a few of the Gothic nobles made a stand, electing one of their number as king. His descendants slowly enlarged their small kingdom and joined with other Christian countries in the Peninsula who were spreading south-wards, first Castile, then Navarre and Aragon. Galicia, which had never been completely subjugated, joined with Leon and Asturias. Combined, they slowly pushed the Moors backwards. The pace of their advance varied according to the strength or weakness of the Moslem conquerors.

In 1037 Fernando I, who had united Leon and Castile, had extended his frontier as far south as the Mondego. The country was again divided on his death, but his son, Alfonso VI, soon turned out his brothers and further enlarged his sovereignty by taking Toledo in 1056. These re-conquests enraged the Moorish powers in Africa, and their fanatical leaders sent armies to the

Peninsula, where they inflicted a great defeat on the Christians at Zalaca. After this disaster and the loss of Lisbon, Alfonso sent a cry for help through Christendom. Many knights came to help him, amongst them Count Raymond of Toulouse and Count Henry of Burgundy. Their help was so successful that the grateful Alfonso gave Raymond his daughter and heiress, Urraca, in marriage, with the kingdom of Galicia as dowry, and to Henry of Burgundy his daughter, Theresa, and the counties of Coimbra and Porto. Thus Portugal, as we know it, was born. Now, for the first time, there was a more or less independent state, which occupied the northern part of the country and took the name of Portugal from the two towns, Portus and Cales, both on the Douro.

Henry of Burgundy spent most of his life fighting, and his new country saw little of him. On his death his widow, Theresa, would not bow to her sister, Urraca, as overlord. Urraca was busy fighting with her second husband, so Theresa had time to consolidate her power and to teach her people to consider themselves as a separate nation, the Portuguese, though at that time there was little difference in race or language between them and the Galicians.

Theresa lost her hold over them, however, when she came too much under the influence of her lover, Dom Fernando Peres de Trava. When Urraca's son, Alfonso Raimond, attacked Theresa, the Portuguese rose and put her son, Affonso Henriques, in her place. Affonso was only eighteen at the time, and after raising an army he fought his cousin, Dom Alfonso of Castile, for the independence of his country. This he finally achieved in 1143 after an ordeal by battle in which a picked band of Portuguese knights defeated the Castilian champions. Then Affonso Henriques declared himself king, and his independence was recognized by Leon and Castile. Affonso Henriques was a great warrior and enlarged his kingdom at the expense of the Moors. He captured many of their great castles and strongholds, which stretched in a long line from one end of the country to the other, and from which the warning of danger could be sent by fire or smoke signals. It was in his reign that the first great epic of Portuguese and English co-operation took place with the capture of Lisbon from the Moors in 1147. Lisbon was at that time a great and rich city. The Moors put its inhabitants at

400,000 to 500,000. Lying on the north bank of the Tagus with its great harbour, it had become the principal European market of the Saracens. The town was dominated by the citadel and the fortification surrounded the city to the shores of the river, which were protected by the Moorish fleet. Even the great soldier Affonso Henriques knew that he could not hope to capture the city without help.

After the defeat of the first Crusade in Asia Minor, the Christians were raising fresh armies to renew their attack on the Infidel.

The large German and French contingents had already started for the Near East overland, following the route of the former Crusaders, but the English, North Germans and those from the Low Countries were maritime nations, and chose the long and, in those days, dangerous journey by sea from the mouths of the Rhine, the Bristol Channel and through the Pillars of Hercules into the Mediterranean.

News of this big, slow-moving fleet must have reached King Affonso, who made his plans accordingly.

There were about 13,000 fighting men in this force, of whom the greatest number were English ("Pars eorum maxima venerat et Anglia"—Henry of Huntingdon). They were joined at Dartmouth by the German Crusaders under Arnulph of Areschot and the Flemings under Christian of Gistell. The English were commanded by four constables. The account of this voyage and the attack on Lisbon was given by an English scholar, a member of the Crusader force, under the title of "Cruce Signati anglici Epist. de expugnatione Ulisiponis." The English contingent reached Oporto first, having lost touch with their German and Flemish companions in a gale.

The Bishop of Oporto received them with great kindness and put before them the king's request that they should join him in an attack on Lisbon and the Moors so comfortably ensconced there. As this was akin to the work they had set out to do, the Crusaders agreed and the fleet set sail for the Tagus, while the king and his army followed overland.

With the great fleet of the Crusaders blockading Lisbon from the sea, the fighting men joined the Portuguese army in surrounding the city on land. The fighting was bitter and hard, and swayed first to one side, then to the other. At last the English managed to take part of the city outside the walls, and with it the grain stores of the garrison, who from then on began to suffer from hunger. The Moors were far more active and clever in the arts of siege warfare than the Christians, and had the advantage for some time. The besiegers were showered with quantities of stones and darts when attacking, for the Saracens had much the stronger machines. A tower built by the English was burned, also another made with great labour by the Germans. The Flemings tried mining on a large scale, but this, too, was countered. At last a huge wooden tower on wheels, designed by a Pisan engineer and made by English and Portuguese, was ready and manned by fifty English and fifty Portuguese. Each one of the hundred was given a piece of the true Cross. This moving castle was rolled up to the city walls, and, in spite of an exceptionally high tide, which cut off help from the besiegers, the tower was pushed nearer and nearer, and finally to within a yard of the battlements. As a drawbridge was put across and the Crusaders were on the point of crossing into the city, the Saracens surrendered ; further resistance was useless.

Affonso's son, Sancho I, consolidated the conquests of his father and restored the country and towns of Beira to prosperity, but it was not until the reign of Affonso III, the grandson of Sancho, that the Moors were finally expelled from the southern part of the country by his conquest of the Algarve in the middle of the thirteenth century.

After him comes one of the great kings of Portuguese history —Diniz the Farmer, or Husbandman. It was to him that Edward of England wrote of the " treaty of love and union that has existed between your merchants and ours." This is the first reference to a treaty between England and Portugal. Diniz it was who planted the belts of pine trees to hold the shifting sands along the coast. He rebuilt many of the great castles, notably that of Leiria. He founded the Knights of Christ, who replaced the Templars at Tomar, and, greatest achievement of all, he brought the still famous university to Coimbra from Lisbon, where it had been founded in 1284, the second earliest university in Europe. It was also during his reign that the order of São Tiago was instituted, who later made the great castle of Palmella their headquarters, where there are still the

arms and names of many English knights, who came to Portugal
to die fighting the Moors. It was he, too, who made the first
commercial treaty with England in 1294. King Diniz' device,
" Que fiz tanto quiz," is perhaps a key to his character, as it
may be freely translated as " I do as I please," and his pleasure
was the consolidation of his country and its growing power.
Now, five centuries later, this, the youngest of those many small
kingdoms of the Iberian Peninsula, is the only one to retain its
separate entity.

The wife of Diniz was Isabel, the beloved Rainha Santa.
Diniz was a careful and rather parsimonious man, and did not
approve of Isabel's many charities. The story is told that when
King Diniz demanded to know what she carried in her basket,
her gifts of bread and food for the poor of Coimbra turned to
flowers. She is buried in the lovely convent of Santa Clara,
opposite Coimbra, across the river Mondego.

Diniz was succeeded by his son, Affonso IV, in 1325, who is
known to history by his cruel murder of Inez de Castro, and
his leadership of the Portuguese troops in the great battle of
Salado, when the Christians inflicted a crushing blow on those
Moors still in the Peninsula. He also made further commercial
treaties with England.

The story of the two great lovers, Inez de Castro and the
king's son, Dom Pedro, has been immortalized in Ferreira's
masterpiece *The Tragedy of Castro*. Dom Pedro had been married
when only sixteen to the Spanish princess, Constanza, daughter
of the Duke of Penafiel. She came to Portugal with a large
train of courtiers and attendants, among them the beautiful
Inez de Castro, daughter of the High Chamberlain of Castile.
The king's son fell deeply in love with Inez. His liaison with
her and one with Dona Theresa Lourenço was not much
thought of during his wife's lifetime, though he had several
children by Inez, and a son, afterwards the great King João I,
by Dona Theresa. When his wife died, he greatly angered
his father by his persistent refusal to marry any of the princesses
pressed upon him for political reasons, and his open and growing
absorption in Inez soon caused jealousy and intrigue at court,
where the Spanish influence of what was supposed to be the
prince's mistress was much resented.

Inez lived in a beautiful house across the river Mondego,

opposite Coimbra, called the Quinta das Lagrimas. Here, by the fountain of love, as it is sometimes called, she was murdered by three knights, at the instigation of the king. There is a deep stain on the stones by the quiet pool—a stain which cannot be destroyed. Her blood, legend says, sank so deeply into the stone that it cannot be removed.

When Pedro heard of her death he broke with his father, attacked and ravaged the Minho and besieged Oporto, but was re-

conciled to him before his death two years later. When Pedro became king he openly acknow-ledged his marriage to Inez and ordered her body to be dis-interred, to be clad in robes of state, and, with a crown on her head, he placed her on the throne beside him. Here the whole court came to do obeis-ance and to kiss her dead hand. He had two of her murderers tortured and killed, while the third escaped to Spain. The body of Inez was carried in state to Alcobaça between two lines of flaming torches held high by the populace. Here she and her royal lover lie in two wonderful tombs. Pedro ordered them to be placed foot to foot, so that on the resur-rection morning they shall rise and find themselves facing each other. These tombs are two of the greatest artistic treasures of Portugal. No one knows who designed them, and they far excel in beauty any other sculpture done both before and even after they were made.

Pedro was succeeded in 1367 by his one legitimate son, Fernando I. Unfortunately Fernando had fallen in love with Dona Leonor Telles de Menezes, wife of a nobleman. He married her though her husband was still alive. At her first court held at Leça, near Oporto, the only one of the Portuguese

FOUNTAIN IN MUSEUM COURT AT COIMBRA

BACALHOA

nobility who refused to acknowledge her as queen was Dom Diniz, the king's half-brother, son of Inez de Castro. Leonor never forgot nor forgave this slight. She was a cruel, evil woman, and was hated for the bad influence she had on the king, and for her vengeance on her own sister, Dona Maria Telles. This sister had married another of Inez de Castro's sons, Dom João, and had had a son, while Leonor's children had died. This added to the hatred Leonor had for all connected with Inez de Castro. She taunted Dom João, telling him that his wife was unfaithful to him, until in a rage he rushed to his house and before she could defend herself killed his wife. The cruel queen then mocked him for believing her, and poor João fled to Castile, after trying to kill the queen in revenge.

Fernando died in 1138, leaving, as his heir, his daughter, Dona Brites, wife of João of Castile, with the cruel Leonor as regent. By now the Portuguese had definitely become an independent nation and had no wish to be absorbed again into Leon and Castile, nor to be ruled by such a woman as Leonor. The people revolted. A Cortes was held at Coimbra, where the son of Dom Pedro and Dona Theresa Lourenço, Dom João, Master of Aviz, was elected king and empowered to raise an army. João I, the Great, as he is often called, fought the Castilian invaders several times and defeated them. The last battle was at Aljubarrota, near Alcobaça, where he finally routed them on 14th August 1386. The arms of the town still carry the baking shovel which commemorates the prowess of the baker's wife who, not to be outdone by the soldiers, spent the day of the battle killing Spaniards with her shovel.

When the Castilian king fled, he left behind all his treasure, amongst this the beautiful silver gilt and enamel triptych and silver angels from the altar, which are now in the museum at Guimarães. Dom João, who had invoked her help before the battle, dedicated all the spoil to Nossa Senhora da Oliveira, and promised, if victorious, to rebuild her church at Guimarães and to found a monastery. The statue of Nossa Senhora was one of the most venerated in Portugal at that date, and had performed many miracles. The legend is that early in the fourteenth century an olive tree grew near the church of S. Torquato, a few miles from Guimarães. The oil from this tree was used for the lamp in front of the Saint's altar. This olive tree was uprooted and brought to Guimarães, where it was replanted opposite the church of Nossa Senhora with the idea of supplying oil for the altar of the Virgin. The tree objected to its transference and died. There it remained, an unsightly relic, until in 1343 a certain Pedro Esteves came to Guimarães and brought with him a cross which his brother had brought from Normandy. Estaves erected the cross beside the dead tree, which three days later sent out green shoots and was soon covered thickly with leaves. The news spread quickly, and the people rushed to see the miracle, which was attributed to the Virgin. The church was known after that as Nossa Senhora da Oliveira and became a place of special pilgrimage. Why that particular tree was moved at all history does not relate. Perhaps it, too, had its story, and may have been the one tradition says grew from the stave of Wamba the Visigoth, who, when chosen king by the people in 672, swore he would not accept office until his stick, which he drove into the ground, should sprout and grow. This it did, and Wamba prayed for help to govern rightly.

With the victory of Aljubarrota the great period of Portuguese history began, and with it an even more intimate connection with England, for the following year the treaty of Windsor was signed, which expressed the close friendship and alliance of the two countries. This alliance was greatly strengthened when John of Gaunt, who claimed Castile for his wife, the daughter of Pedro the Cruel, landed in Galicia with a large army and marched to meet Dom João at Oporto in February 1387. After this the marriage was celebrated between João and his daughter Philippa of Lancaster. John of Gaunt gave up all claim to Galicia when he married the daughter of his second wife, Constance of Castile, to Enrique, Prince of the Asturias ; so peace came to the Peninsula.

During the fifty years of his reign, João saw his country rise to consequence and glory. He was greatly helped by his energetic but quick-tempered wife. Between them they built the beautiful Abbey of Batalha, where they lie in the Founder's Chapel surrounded by the tombs of their sons. During this reign the great period of Portuguese expansion oversea began by the capture, with the help of English archers and men-at-arms, of Ceuta on the African coast opposite Gibraltar. The king's fourth son, Prince Henry, afterwards known as the

Navigator, showed great courage in this battle, and from then devoted his life and the huge fortune of the Knights of Christ, of which he was the Grand Master, to the encouragement of maritime ventures. Madeira was reached in 1419, the Azores in 1434, Cape Verde in 1446. He built an observatory at Sagres, near Cape St. Vincent, and founded there a school of discovery. The trade with West Africa greatly increased as he sent his adventurers along the coast in search of a way to reach Prester John. Thus he added to Portuguese possessions and to her fortunes through the slave trade, which was then a great source of profit. The first negro brought to Europe from Central Africa came to the town of Lagos. There is a record of one being sent to the little church at Cape St. Vincent and becoming a Franciscan friar. Before his death in 1460 Prince Henry saw Portugal in the way of becoming one of the greatest colonial powers.

The sole setback which they suffered during this period was the unsuccessful attack on Tangiers, when his youngest brother, Dom Fernando the Infante Santo, was taken prisoner and died six years later, having consistently refused to obtain his release by the return of Ceuta to the Moors. João I was succeeded by his son, Duarte, who only reigned the five years from 1433 to 1438, and his son, Affonso V, reaped the benefits of his Uncle Henry's courageous vision and enterprise, for it was during his reign that many of the discoveries already mentioned were made, as well as the capture of Tangiers and Arzila in the wars of 1458–71. João II, who followed Affonso, saw Diogo Cão discover the Congo, Bartolomeu Diaz get to Cape Tormentoso, as he called it at first, for he was turned back by adverse winds, but Cape of Good Hope, when he finally rounded it and opened the new way to India and the Far East. Other adventurers besides the Portuguese had been searching the unknown seas in the hopes of finding an easier way to the lands of spices and riches, for in those days all the Eastern trade came by caravan over the long and dangerous land route.

Christopher Columbus was one of them. He stopped in Portugal on his way back from his discovery of America in 1492. The Portuguese were in two minds as to what they would do with him. They wanted no poaching on their preserves of world discovery and exploration. Should they put him quietly out of the way or let him go on his way to Spain ? The plague was raging in Lisbon at the time, and Christopher was told to go to Valparaiso to meet the king and recount his adventures. This he did, and the church where he stayed is still in existence, though partly in ruins. The councillors of the day came to the conclusion that what Columbus had discovered would in no way conflict with Portugal's growing empire. They had rounded the Cape of Good Hope in 1486, although Vasco da Gama did not find the sea route to India until five years after Columbus had discovered America. They felt that the wild country which Columbus told of held less for them than did their own discoveries, so they let him pass on to Spain and lost the gold of Peru and Mexico. It was not until Pedro Alvares Cabral discovered Brazil in 1500 that their interest was kindled, and they then added this huge tract of country to their empire.

João II, dying in 1495, was succeeded by his cousin, Manuel I, the Fortunate. The Golden Age of Portugal came to its zenith under him. It was he who sent Vasco da Gama to search out the sea route to India in 1497. Before he sailed on this great adventure, Vasco da Gama spent the night in prayer at the shrine of Nossa Senhora at Belem. It was here that the king later built the great church and convent of Jeronimos in grati-tude for his return and the riches he brought with him. Da Gama reached Calicut on the Malabar coast nearly a year after he had left Lisbon. When he returned he brought a letter from the ruler or *Zamorin* to Dom Manuel : " Vasco da Gama, a nobleman of thy household, has visited my kingdom and given me much pleasure. In my kingdom is abundance of cinnamon, cloves, ginger, pepper and precious stones. What I seek from thy country is gold, silver, coral and scarlet " (from Danvers' *Portuguese in India*, vol. i.). The return of da Gama and his ships laden with treasure in July 1499 was the cause of much rejoicing. He was given a large sum of money, a title and

pension, and the crews shared in the good fortune, though only
ninety-six of the original hundred and forty-eight had returned.
From then Lisbon became the European centre of the spice
trade, perhaps the most valuable in the world at that date.
The king is supposed to have made a profit of sixty to one after
all expenses were paid on the first expedition.

Manuel fitted out another expedition to repeat da Gama's
success. This time the leader was Pedro Alvares Cabral, who
sailed from Lisbon with thirteen ships in March 1500. High
winds drove him out of his course, and after many days he
sighted welcome land, and found he had discovered a great new
continent. He landed and took possession of it in the name of
Portugal, leaving a cross in memory of his visit. Thus Brazil
was added to the growing list of Portuguese colonies. Sending
back the news to Lisbon by one of his ships, Cabral made for the
Cape of Good Hope and reached Calicut in September, having
lost some of his ships in a gale on the way. He was not as well
received as da Gama had been, and after a fight with Arab
traders, who killed some of his men, he burned part of the town
and sailed for Cochin, where he was made very welcome. He
had only three of his ships left when he got back to Lisbon.

The greatest of all these sailor adventurers was Affonso
Albuquerque, the admiral and viceroy who followed closely
on the heels of da Gama and Cabral. He was a man of extraordinary ability and force of character, and added more lustre
to Manuel's reign. He greatly extended the power of Portugal
in India and the East from 1503 to 1515, capturing Goa, which
he made his capital, in 1510, the islands of Ormez and Malacca
in 1513, subduing Malabar, Ceylon and other parts of the
East before he died, worn out by his great exertions, in 1515.
He was a great loss to the nation, for after him no one came
who added as many possessions or gave as much power to their
country as did Albuquerque in his twelve years as viceroy.
Manuel also saw Peres de Andrade reach China in 1517,
occupy Macao and, before that, the volcanic islands in the
South Atlantic were discovered by Tristan da Cunha in 1506.
Ferdinand Magellan, or, to give him his Portuguese name, Fernão
de Magalhães, was another of the great explorers whom the foresight of Henry the Navigator had encouraged, and he followed in
the footsteps of his great predecessors—fighting with distinction

in Malacca and the Indies under Alburquerque, and also in
Africa. Then for some reason he displeased the king, so it
was as a Portuguese flying the flag of the emperor, Charles V,
that he sailed in 1519 for Brazil, where he suppressed a rising
in San Julian and afterwards discovered the straits which are
called after him. He crossed the Pacific, which he named, and
was killed in a fight with the natives of Malan in the Philippines.

The glory and riches brought to Portugal by her sons was in
those days even greater than those of Spain. This Golden Age
added not only possessions but many domestic treasures. The
great Castle of the Knights Templar and then of the Knights
of Christ at Tomar was added to and enriched, a fitting memorial
to its former Grand Master, Henry the Navigator, the man of
vision and determination, to whom the world as well as Portugal
owes so much. San Jeronimos was built at Belem, Manuel
employing João de Castilo, the architect who had helped
to add to Tomar. At Belem the completely Portuguese type of
architecture called Manueline is shown at its most distinctive.
There is nothing like it in any other country, while at Tomar
the severe Gothic of the early structure is overlaid by the florid
Renaissance work to which João de Castilo had been converted.
There is fine church plate which dates from that period, as well
as some earlier, for Portugal had always been the home of the
craftsman in gold and silver.

The decline of this great age had already begun in the reign
of João III, 1521–57, for the drain on her man-power by the
plague at home and the emigration to her colonies had been
great. Her population had never been large, and Prince Henry
had only one million souls to call upon for his great schemes
of world discovery and colonization. We can look with wonder
and admiration at what a small nation had done with vision,
courage and enterprise. Alas ! she suffered for it, for the best
were those who risked their lives to add jewels to their national
crown, and many did not return from their adventures. Another
cause of decline was the expulsion of the Jews, which began in
1507, as well as the establishment of the Inquisition in Lisbon
in 1536.

In 1557 Sebastian, the Desired, succeeded his grandfather.
He saw the rise of the national poet, Luis de Camoens, who
wrote of da Gama's great exploits in the *Lusiad*. To Sebastian

fanatically proud of the valour of his countrymen and of their
share in the expulsion of the Moslem from Europe, the fact that
the Moors were still in Morocco, so near to southern Portugal,
was a perpetual irritation.   He begged his uncle, Philip II of
Spain, to join him in a crusade to capture Morocco for the Cross,
but Philip was in no position to help.   He was nearly bankrupt,
and in trouble with both Elizabeth of England and the Flemings.
He also feared to rouse Islam against himself, so he refused
Sebastian's request and did his best to stop the foolish expedition,
but Sebastian was bent on his conquest and filled with Christian
zeal.   He took his army across the straits against the wishes,
and to the great sorrow, of his people.   Here he and his army
were routed in the battle of Alcazar Kebir on 4th August 1578.
His fate is unknown, for his body was never found.   His heir
was his old great-uncle, Cardinal Dom Henrique, who lived for
under two years as king, leaving to five regents the choice of
his successor.   There were several claimants, the most popular
Dom Antonio, Prior of Crato, the doubtfully legitimate grandson of Manuel.   The rightful heir should have been the Duchess
of Braganza, daughter of Manuel's youngest son.   Philip II saw
in the vacant throne of Portugal the chance to redress his fortunes.
The great wealth of the Portuguese crown would enable him
by force of power and money to crush his enemies, for all his
failures in the past had been for the lack of means.   With
Portugal would come the wealth of the East Indies, where the
Portuguese were rapidly ousting the Venetians.   Brazil, Africa,
would give him far greater riches than any other European king.
Philip had bribed three of the regents left by the old king, and
the Portuguese nobility were either bribed or taken to Spain.
Philip sent Alva to take his army through the country with
hardly any opposition, except from Antonio's forces, which were
defeated in two battles.   The unfortunate Pretender fled, and
Philip received the oath of allegiance from the Portuguese
Cortes at Tomar on 1st April 1581.   Only Elizabeth of England
and a frightened Catherine de Medici remained to stand between
him and the world power he craved.

The sixty years of the Spanish captivity had begun and
lasted until 1640.   Philip placed the Austrian archduke, Cardinal
Albert, as regent in Portugal.   The harsh rule of Spain under
him and Philip III and IV caused great discontent in Portugal.

Philip II had respected her constitution, but under the following reigns the country became spoil for the Spanish, and Portuguese offices, bishoprics and viceroyalties were given to Spanish adherents of the current favourite. In other ways Portugal suffered from her connection with Spain. Her ships were no longer safe from Spanish enemies, and much of the Lisbon trade had been directed to Cadiz. There was also a complete dearth of artistic work.

When in 1636 Olivares, the king's favourite, put a 5 per cent. tax on all property, the smouldering rebellion broke out. It was soon suppressed, and the regent, the Duchess of Mantua, Philip IV's first cousin, did her best to undo the harm, but it was too late. Olivares then decreed that a further tax should be imposed, and even announced that the Cortes would be abolished and that Portugal would return to her status of centuries ago, that of a county of Castile. This was too much for the proud nation, and a large party gathered round the Duke of Braganza, the principal candidate for the throne. His wife was an able, forceful Spanish woman of the great house of the Dukes of Medina and Sidonia. Efforts were made by Spain to bribe Braganza by the offers of viceroyalties, but he refused to move, even when ordered to Madrid. Several attempts were made to capture him, but safe amongst his people he remained. At last in November 1640 his supporters and his wife prevailed on Braganza to proclaim himself king. On 1st December a small body of nobles and soldiers surprised the palace, and the populace hailed Braganza as the saviour of the country. He was still in the country, but was at once proclaimed João IV of Portugal, and after a three hours' revolt against little opposition Portugal was free from Castile, never again to be her vassal. No one dared to bring the news to Philip, fearing Olivares' anger and vengeance, until the favourite himself sugared the bitter pill. "Albricias, Albricias, Your Majesty, good news. You have won a great Duchy and a great estate." " How ? " asked the king. " The Duke of Braganza has gone mad and proclaimed himself king of Portugal, so that you may seize the twelve million ducats' worth of property that he owns." The sixty years of captivity had ended.

João had a difficult reign in many ways. He was continually at war with Spain, and though he got support from Charles of

England, the Parliamentarians were unfriendly. Prince Rupert
and his cavalier fleet sheltered in the Tagus while Blake, the
Parliamentarian admiral, blockaded the port, but through it
all João preserved a just neutrality. For many years he tried
through France, with the promise of aid by Mazarin, to make
a truce with Spain and to have his independence acknowledged.
Mazarin played his own game, and in spite of bribes did little
to help João and Portugal. It was not until 1668, during the
reign of Affonso VI and the regency of his brother, Dom Pedro,
that peace was at last secured with the help of England, with
whom there were closer ties than ever as Charles II had married
Affonso's sister, Catherine of Braganza. Affonso had been
married by proxy to Mademoiselle d'Aumale, but on her arrival
in Portugal the marriage was dissolved and she married instead
the Infante Dom Pedro. Poor half-paralysed Affonso was
imprisoned by his brother, who became regent, and Affonso
died in 1683. Many suspected foul play.

Pedro, his brother and regent, became king. During his
reign the great Brazilian gold-fields were discovered and riches
again poured into the country, but principally into the king's
pocket. In 1701 the British fleet well-nigh destroyed the French
and Spanish in Vigo Bay, and two years later the Methuen
treaty was signed with England, when mutual trade benefits
were exchanged. Pedro was succeeded by his son, João V,
who spent lavishly the huge fortune pouring in from Brazil.
He helped Portuguese craftsmanship by inducing Chippendale
to go there, where, for two years, he was official cabinetmaker
to the court. As most Portuguese furniture is still hand-made
the tradition left by Chippendale has remained. His models
were much copied. João, delighted at the birth of a son, built
the huge monastery and Palace of Mafra, on which he is supposed
to have spent four million pounds. The financial ruin of the
country was nearly complete when this spendthrift king, known
as the Magnificent, died and was followed by his son, José.

Though the new king was thirty-six when he came to the
throne, he knew little of his country's affairs and was indeed
lucky in one of the ministers, which his mother, the queen, had
recalled from his post as Ambassador to London and Vienna to
become Minister for Foreign Affairs. The Marquez de Pombal,
by which name he is best known, was about fifty when he took

office. He soon had complete ascendancy over the new king, and together they started on the difficult task of restoring prosperity and life to the country. Pombal showed great strength of character and energy. He enjoyed the complete confidence and backing of the king during his lifetime. He had many obstacles to overcome, opposition from both Church and nobility and the people's prejudices. He curbed the power of the Inquisition. No *auto-da-fé* was to take place without the government's consent. He put his country's defences into condition and did much to help industry and agriculture. The laws were enforced and the streets of Lisbon, hitherto unsafe, were cleaned and policed. He made many and great economies, and the country's finances were put in order. A decree in 1755 declared all the native Indians in parts of Brazil free, and he sent his brother there to see that this was carried out. The terrible earthquake of November 1755 interrupted these reforms, but confirmed Pombal in the king and country's esteem, for he worked day and night, visiting the scenes of devastation, helping the wounded, burying the dead, which numbered nearly thirty thousand. Under him Lisbon rose again, a city of fine squares and good buildings. England sent £100,000 to help the sufferers, and this again drew the two countries closer. Pombal broke the power of the Jesuits and put their great school under secular direction, while he started over eight hundred elementary schools in the country. To break the power of the nobles he imprisoned many of them, so that when José died in 1777 and his daughter, Maria I, who was married to her uncle, Dom Pedro, became queen, he quickly fell from power, for his imprisoned enemies were released and the court was filled with his foes. The queen, urged on by her mother, who had never forgiven Pombal for the fall of the Jesuits, dismissed the aged Minister, and he retired to his estate, where he died in 1782. His reforms were continued by the queen, who founded the Royal Academy of Science in 1779. However, she had shown signs of religious mania, and when her husband, Dom Pedro, died, and shortly afterwards her eldest son, Dom José, to be followed by the death of her confessor and guide, Ignacio de San Galtano, she became quite mad. Her second son became regent and afterwards king on her death in 1816.

In the meantime a great star had risen to the North-East.

Napoleon was consolidating his great conquests and placing his family on the various thrones of Europe. He demanded the closing of the Portuguese ports to the ships of his enemy, England, and the seizing of all British property in Portugal and he sent Junot to enforce his demands ; but the regent had asked the help of England, and on 2nd November 1807 the court, the treasure, archives of state, many ministers and courtiers set sail for Brazil under the protection of the British Fleet. When Junot's ragged and starving army arrived in Lisbon they found the capital empty of all value.

From then on the domestic history of Portugal was that of the British armies in the Peninsular Wars. During these terrible years this small and unarmed country rose to great heights of sacrifice and courage when, on Wellington's orders, the people destroyed all their food and possessions, leaving Massena to march through empty and hungry country until he was beaten, first at Busaco by the much smaller English army and its Portuguese contingents. Later he was forced to retreat from Torres Vedras after months of starvation and harrying by militia which had been left in his rear.

The lines at Torres Vedras behind which Wellington had retreated with the whole population of the invaded districts were kept a complete secret from Massena, though hundreds of Portuguese had been at work on them for months. Massena first knew of their existence a few days before his army reached them, and their tremendous strength and depth prevented his making any direct assault, though he made two attacks on outlying positions.

When peace came, after the Congress of Vienna, King João VI returned to Lisbon in 1822 to reign for a short time under the new constitution, which had been promulgated in 1820. When he died in 1826 his eldest son, Dom Pedro, remained in Brazil, first as regent then as emperor, appointing his daughter, Maria, Queen of Portugal. However, her uncle, Dom Miguel the regent, had himself proclaimed king. He was not challenged until Dom Pedro returned to Lisbon in 1831, having abdicated in favour of his six-year-old son, and left him Emperor of Brazil. After much fighting Miguel was finally defeated at Evora Monte in 1834, and Pedro took over the regency for his daughter, but died a few months later. His short dictatorship left much good behind it, for his many decrees brought freedom to the land, and when Maria II started her reign, the semi-feudal Portugal of history had disappeared. Her troubled reign ended in 1853, and her son, Pedro, succeeded her under the regency of his father, Ferdinand of Saxe-Coburg, brother of Prince Albert, Prince Consort of England. Pedro's reign was short, for he died of yellow fever caught while helping his people when the plague came to Lisbon. His brother, Dom Luis, succeeded him in 1861 and died in 1889. His queen, Maria Pia, was the fountain of much charity and of many good works, and her memory is much loved.

King Charles, their son, was murdered with his eldest son in 1908, after a reign of many hopes frustrated by corruption in politics and great extravagance on the king's part. His son, King Manuel, only reigned for two years, when the ferment in the country and republican feeling became too strong for him to remain on the throne. He fled to England, where he died a few years later. The Republic, so much longed for, was established in 1910, and at first had a rough passage, with many monarchist and radical risings and with the murder of President Sidonio Pais in 1918. Peace did not come to the faction-torn country until General Carmona became President in 1926. He was joined by Dr. Salazar in 1928.

Portugal has played a great and useful part in the World War, and her centuries-old friendship for England has been of great value to us. Her many friends look forward and hope that her future will be as great as her past.

Long may she be the land of beauty, promise and pleasure to the tired citizens of less happy countries.

A SHORT LIST OF THE MOST IMPORTANT BOOKS
CONSULTED

The Royal Power and the Cortes, by E. Prestage (Watford, 1925).

The Diplomatic Relations of Portugal, 1640–1668, by E. Prestage (Watford, 1925).

The Portuguese Pioneers, by E. Prestage (1932).

Journal in Portugal, by Mrs. Quillinan (London, 1847).

Portugal Old and New, by Oswald Crawford (London, 1882).

Portugal, by Rodney Gallop (London, 1936).

Beckford's *Italy, Spain and Portugal* (London, 1840).

Portuguese Architecture, by W. Crum Watson (London, 1908).

The Legacy of Islam, by Professor J. B. Trant, Oxford.

Portugal in Quest of Prester John, by Elaine Sanceau (London, 1944).

The Memoirs of Jacome Ratton (London, 1813).

Spanish Baroque Art, by Sacheverell Sitwell (London, 1931).

Pombal, by Marcus Cheke (London).

The Golden Bough, by Fraser, 3rd ed. (London, 1936).

Cambridge Modern History (Cambridge, 1902–10).

History of Garden Art, by M. L. Gothein, translated by L. Archer-Hind (London, 1928).

Flora de Portugal, by Professor Coutinho (Lisbon, 1913).

Palacio National do Queluz, by Caldeira a Pires (Coimbra, 1924).

Palacio e Quinta de Bacalhoa in Azeitão, by Rasteiro (Lisbon, 1895).

Prince Henry the Navigator, by C. Raymond Beazley (London, 1901).

Indies Adventure, the Career of Afonso de Albuquerque, by Elaine Sanceau (London, 1936).

Portinho. 26
Troia   26 - 8 Cetobriga
Castle of Palmella. 26
Villa Fresca de Azeitão
          C of São Simão 64

  Palacio of Bacalhao 64 - 6
      Queluz 68 - 9
Matens - near Vila Real p 72 barope
Convento da Serra d'Ossa 75.6   m Retando
Alcobaca - 14 C Tombs   Dom Pedro I e Inez da Castro
  ,, largest Cistercian Abbey 1148 - 1227